nidgsguirwayhsoak

This book is dedicated to Ruthie, Danielle and Evan
who have always supported me,
through the tough years and late nights. It's their book too.

I also want to acknowledge all of the talented people I've had the good fortune
to work with over the years.
I will always value their friendships and
contributions to my studio.

soakwashrinsespin

TOLLESON DESIGN

Princeton Architectural Press, New York

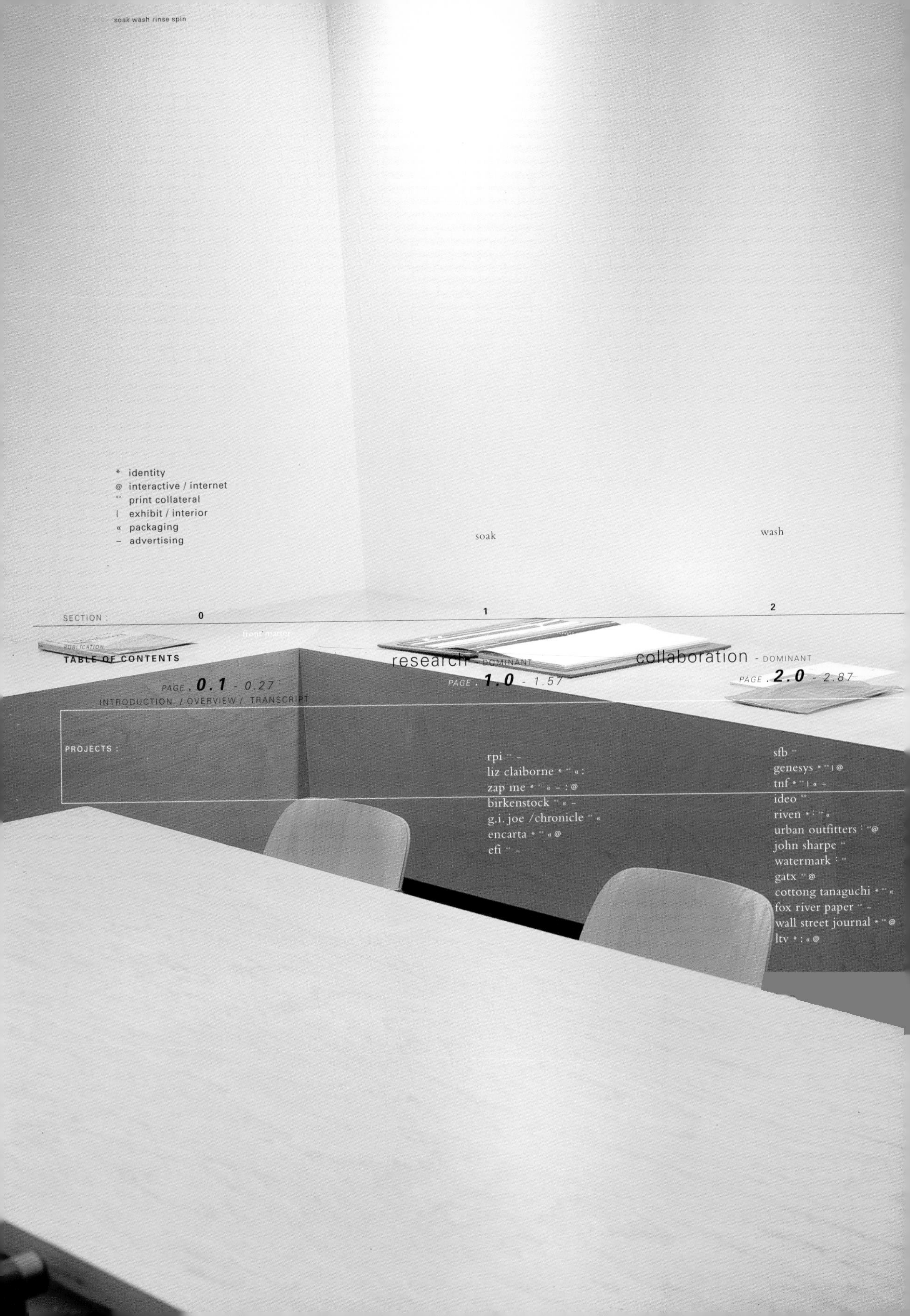

soak wash rinse spin

* identity
@ interactive / internet
" print collateral
| exhibit / interior
« packaging
– advertising

soak

wash

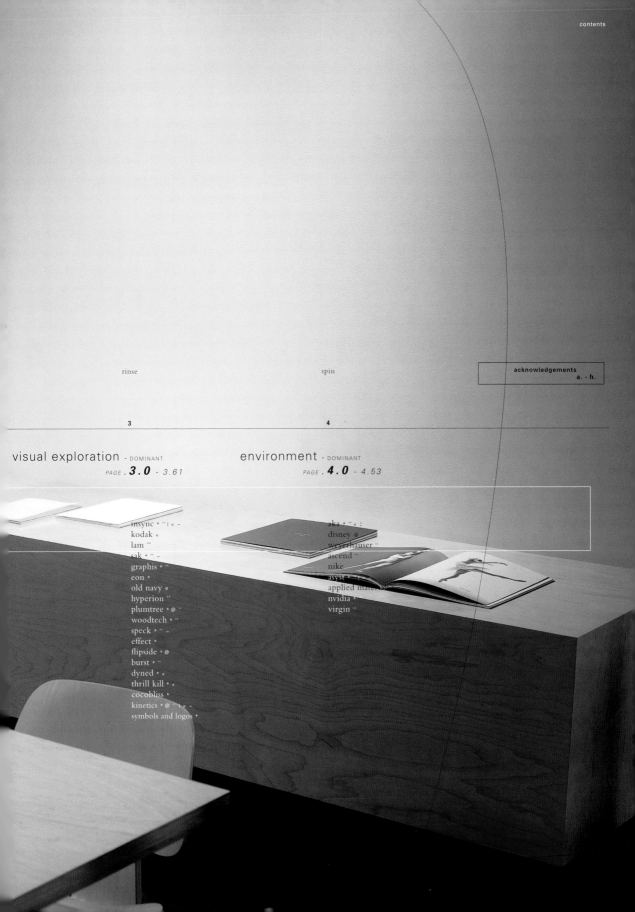

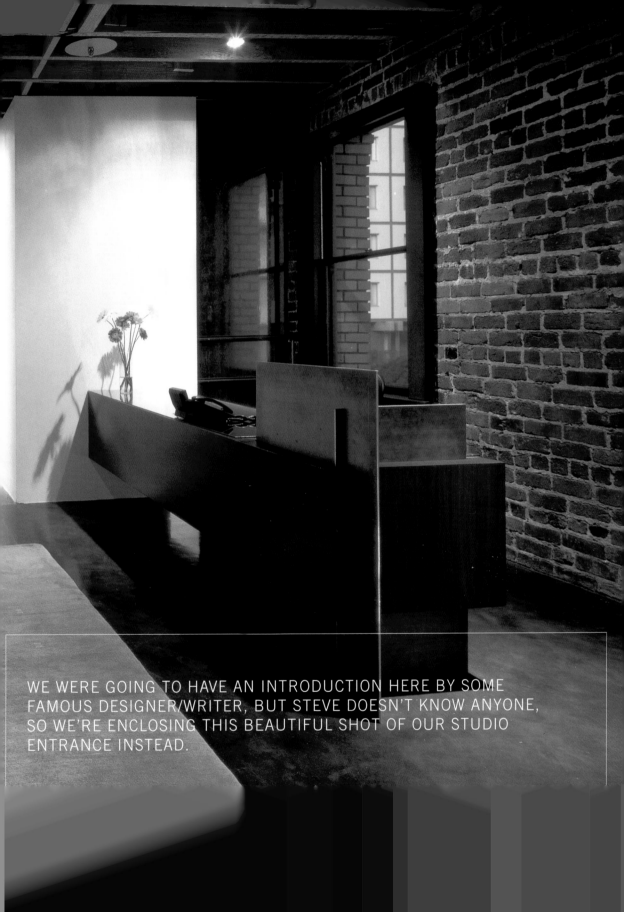

WE WERE GOING TO HAVE AN INTRODUCTION HERE BY SOME
FAMOUS DESIGNER/WRITER, BUT STEVE DOESN'T KNOW ANYONE,
SO WE'RE ENCLOSING THIS BEAUTIFUL SHOT OF OUR STUDIO
ENTRANCE INSTEAD.

THE PROCESS ——

When we began discussing this project with Princeton Architectural Press, I wanted
the book to do several things. Among them, I wanted to illustrate what actually goes
on in my studio, especially in terms of our particular working environment and process.
I wanted to provide real insights into how we work and the types of issues we deal with
that affect a project — things like the mix of communication goals, the corporate culture,
concepts, and ideas of our clients, or the effects of a given medium.

Each project has its own, truly individual story. Every project is a good one, no matter
what its size, schedule, budget, or subject. By offering a candid view of the process
behind a few dozen projects of various types, we hope to take the reader beyond just
the visual content, and into the solution itself. This process is inherently dynamic, and
often distinctly nonlinear, but one which is influenced by everyone involved — on both
the client and designer side of the table. By revealing the communication challenge both
designers and clients face, I hope to illustrate my conviction that the best outcomes
are rooted more in business considerations than they are in just visual explorations.

Despite its whimsy, the book's title is a useful metaphor that defines our studio process.
It also provides the organizing principles for the book's four sections.

SOAK: The first phase in every project is research. No matter what the project size and
scope, we start with an intensive homework phase. It entails just about anything it takes
to get our hands around the client's business:
reading previous collateral, interviewing within
the company, analyzing competitive materials,
reviewing business and marketing plans,
perusing IPO prospectuses, understanding the
brand, as well as familiarizing ourselves with
the client's overall industry trends and issues.
All told, it is an order of magnitude of more
information than can possibly fit into the end
product. But it is essential for providing
context, understanding messages, and being
aware of the target audience's self-interest.

1.   research
2.   collaboration
3.   visual exploration
4.   environment

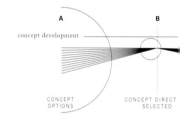

concept development

A   B

CONCEPT   CONCEPT DIRECT
OPTIONS   SELECTED

WASH: The second step is a very collaborative stage among everyone involved. This is
a two-part wash cycle — external and internal. Externally, we invite the client into the
process as an active participant — even before any specific ideas coalesce. They help
us navigate through this research phase, then sit in on very preliminary presentations —
mostly to provide reactions to a spectrum of approaches. This stage is less about design
than it is about thinking together through concepts. Internally, we assemble the entire
cast of studio characters, who have all been involved in the research review, and we
conduct extremely uninhibited idea sessions. We don't limit these sessions to just the
core group of designers, because I like everyone involved to understand the project
scope and goals. Not only for the brainstorming, but also to be informed in the critique
sessions we have before formal client presentations. We apply a wealth of talent with
different perspec-tives and ideas, which makes the outcome a collective effort.

While each project, customer and solution are unique, the process that we employ is consistent each time. The diagram illustrates the way we approach any new challenge. Beginning with a wide range of options, we work to focus the solution down to one particular direction, which is then opened up to more in-depth exploration. This way, the result we achieve is looked at from all angles, considered in every detail.

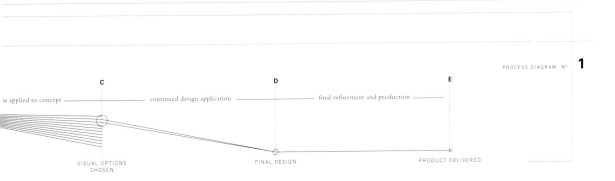

PROCESS DIAGRAM. N° **1**

C   D   E

is applied to concept ——————— continued design application ——————— final refinement and production ———————

VISUAL OPTIONS
CHOSEN

FINAL DESIGN

PRODUCT DELIVERED

Fortunately I learned a long time ago that a really successful project has nothing to do with the way something looks. A successful project is one where everybody involved feels good about the process. We are almost never happy with the final product because there are always so many "if onlys". But a successful project means that both the client and the designer feel equal ownership of the result. They both have made significant contributions that influenced the final product. That it was a joint effort, a beneficial relationship, and an enjoyable process.

THE PROCESS

RINSE: Here we take the WASH and begin an extensive visual exploration of how to render or translate the concepts that have emerged in the previous stages. In this phase, it is critical to suspend judgment, so that we never rule out a design path that may lead to yet another more viable solution. By applying design without preconception about specific styles, we let ideas articulate themselves visually without the inhibitions related to schedule and budget.

SPIN: In this final step, we consider the environment, how the outcome of the project is perceived in its final context. As we explore various design paths, we further refine our ideas by plugging in where and how the piece will be presented to its intended audience. Is it for a retail consumer or another business? Does it exist in a digital format, reside inside a box, print on a page, or hang off a garment? This phase ensures that, when the design piece is passed along, whether it's picked up off the Internet or a shelf, we have anticipated the desired end result and how the graphic treatment can

There is some point, after all the thinking and planning and brainstorming and sketching, that something just starts to look right. Yet I never know if it would have looked right without all of the thinking and planning and brainstorming and sketching. I think you have to get to the point where your intuition is informed.

support or bring about the end effect. So when all is said and done, the final piece works in as effective and efficient a manner as possible for the client. This is my studio's process, what makes us who we are. It remains consistent for clients from start-ups to Fortune 100 companies. It doesn't change depending on the business category, or the size of the piece, or the print run, or even the brevity of the deadline. And even though we identify it as a process, we always experience it with a sense of discovery and satisfaction. We don't mean to say that this is the best, or even the only way to design. But I hope that there is something here for you to enjoy, whether it is appreciating the design, recognizing a similar experience, generating a new idea, or even just having a good laugh.

It's a huge commitment, a lifetime actually, to care for a studio like it's a child, to worry constantly, to love it too, to never forget it for a minute.

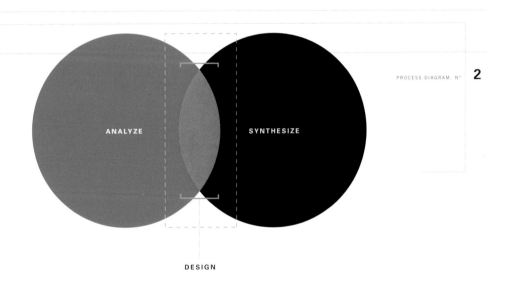

PROCESS DIAGRAM. N° **2**

BOOK LEGEND

The pages of this book are formatted in a manner similar to a set of presentation drawings. The header at the top identifies pertinent project information — name, title, number, etc. — and provides a context for the images that follow.

N° 117   TOLLESON DESIGN

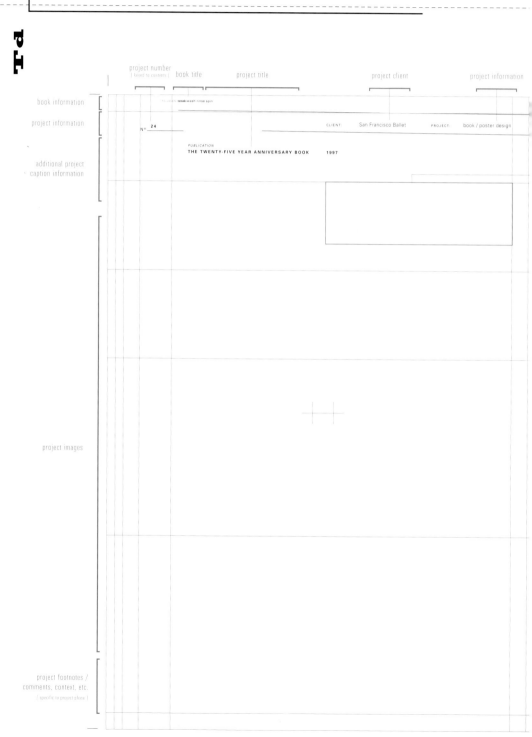

book information

project information

additional project
caption information

project images

project footnotes /
comments, context, etc.
[specific to project phase]

project number
[keyed to contents]   book title   project title   project client   project information

TOLLESON soak wash rinse spin

N° 24   CLIENT: San Francisco Ballet   PROJECT: book / poster design

PUBLICATION
THE TWENTY-FIVE YEAR ANNIVERSARY BOOK   1997

CLIENT: Princeton Architectural Press   PROJECT: TD book   SPECIFIC: layout legend   DATE: 12.18.98

DIR. N° **3.°**

project design direction number
[keyed to project diagram]

caption information

book section and page number

book section

book information

3.**19**

visual exploration

DIR. N°   **1**.0 - **2**.2

project information

additional project
caption information

project images

project footnotes /
comments, context, etc.
[specific to project phase]

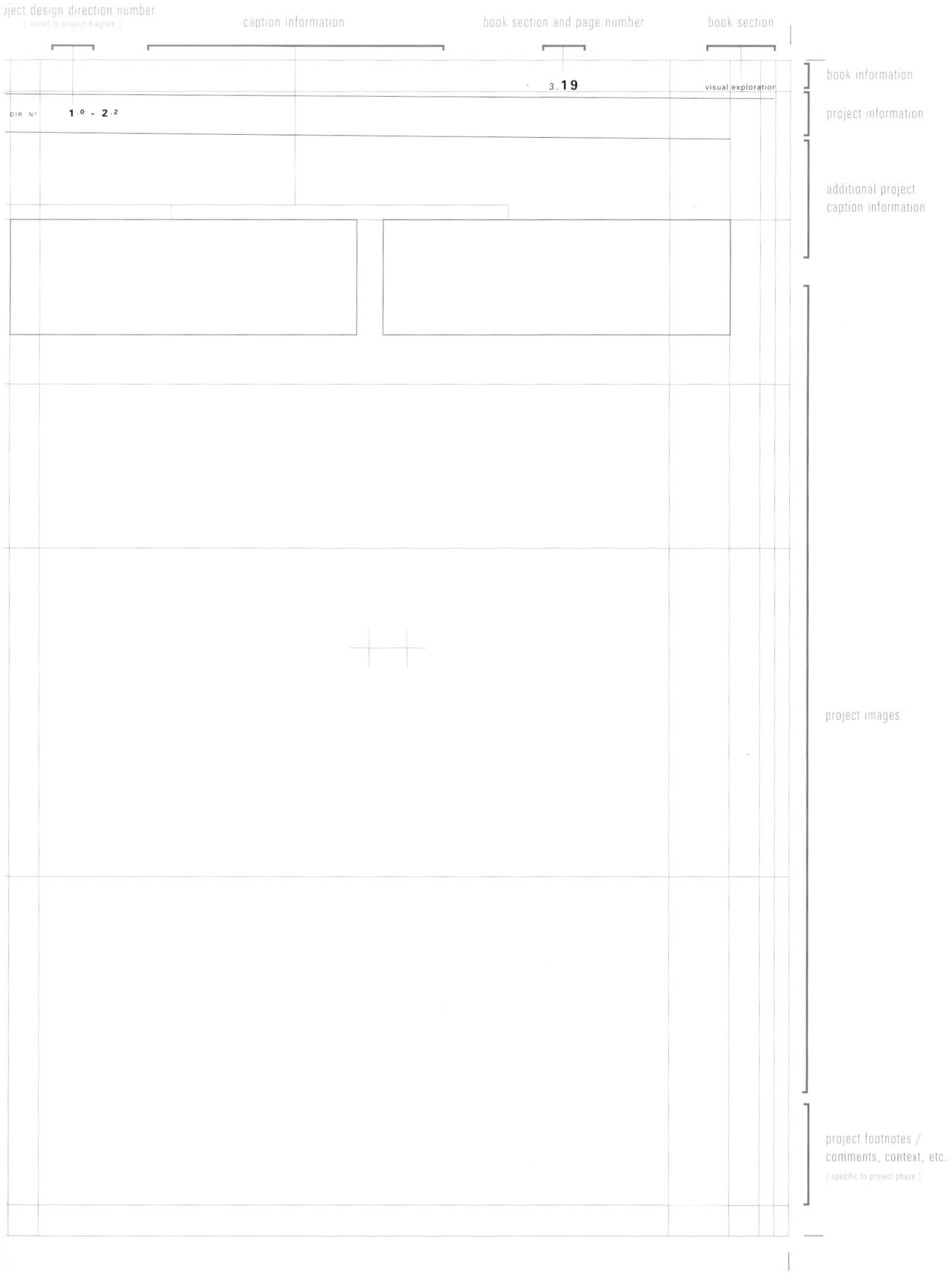

THE CRIT WALL

I-TD/INTRO (1-27)
6.29.99 -

I first opened my doors in 1984. Actually, it was my San Francisco apartment, in which the bedroom doubled as the studio. That location lasted nine months, followed by a succession of progressively larger spaces until, almost 16 years later, we occupy our present space on the edge of San Francisco's Financial District. There are 14 people in the studio, including 7 designers, with support in production and technology, accounting, project management, finance and office management. We also usually have an intern, a tradition from my teaching days.

Design is the latest in a string of jobs I've held since I began fending for myself. Fortunately, it's also the one I've been with the longest. I met one of my earliest and

1981	1982	1983	1984	1985
	6.		1.	6.	1.
	BFA FINE ARTS, GRAPHIC DESIGN, CSUC [CHICO]		OPENED STUDIO	GOT MARRIED	PRINCIPAL'S SALAR $20,000

most important influences in high school when I studied art for four years with a teacher named Ken Waterstreet. A dedicated teacher and a well-known California artist, Ken introduced me to just about everything having to do with fine art: drawing, painting, sketching, color, technique, textures, and scale. And just as exciting to a teenager, back in the 70s, Ken knew all the leading artists like Ralph Goings, Jasper Johns, Klaus Oldenburg, Roy Lichtenstein, Wayne Thiebaud, and others. He often took me to some of these artists' studios, where I spoke with them and looked at their work. That experience has always stayed with me.

Fine art fascinated me as an outlet of personal expression, a release and translation of emotions and experience onto a permanent medium. Also, I liked how fine art is ultimately subjective, internally oriented, meant to please no one but the artist. I majored in fine art in college, and continued to take a lot of art classes, but my paintings concentrated on huge canvases, 10 to 12 feet square and larger. I was doing photorealism-type paintings that rendered abstract detail objects in all different kinds of media. The images were complex, detailed, colorful, and took a great deal of time to complete — as well as tremendous patience.

It wasn't until I had to design a poster for a visiting artist exhibit at school that I first encountered graphic design. As a fine artist, I did not have a clue about how to design a poster; I had never worked with type, knew nothing about production, and was completely ignorant about printing. I asked one of the design faculty for help, and was hooked. As I went through my first graphic design project, I was really struck by the contrast it provided to the slow pace of my large-scale fine art. Graphic design provided an instant gratification for an external audience on a much more human scale. Yet it still applied what I love about fine art.

If I could do it all over again, I would only change a couple of things.

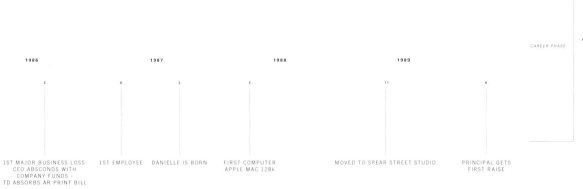

CAREER PHASE

1

| 1986 | 1987 | 1988 | 1989 |

3. 8. 3. 3. 11. 6.

1ST MAJOR BUSINESS LOSS: 1ST EMPLOYEE   DANIELLE IS BORN   FIRST COMPUTER   MOVED TO SPEAR STREET STUDIO   PRINCIPAL GETS
CEO ABSCONDS WITH   APPLE MAC 128k   FIRST RAISE
COMPANY FUNDS -
TD ABSORBS AR PRINT BILL

My absolute worst new business experience: I drove miles and miles I don't remember
where to see some potential client. He was hungry; said "lets do this over lunch." He
meant his lunch. We sat in a booth at a diner and I tried to present my portfolio around
his food. He didn't say a word. I tried to talk continuously so it wouldn't be awkward.
I never heard from him.

My wife is a nurse in newborn intensive care. It helps keep things in perspective. I'm sure it's why I don't get stressed out about schedules.

The absolute most challenging thing is to do something simple. Because simple has to be perfect. If it's not perfect you see it a mile away. It's easier to create something complex, which of course can be really interesting to look at, but for me, always feels like a more subjective solution.

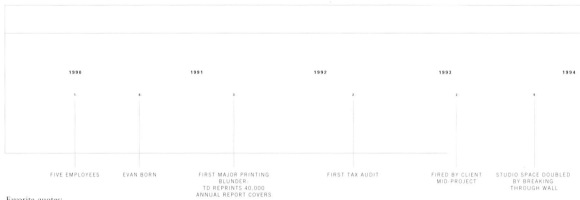

1990	1991	1992	1993	1994
FIVE EMPLOYEES	EVAN BORN	FIRST MAJOR PRINTING BLUNDER: TD REPRINTS 40,000 ANNUAL REPORT COVERS	FIRST TAX AUDIT	FIRED BY CLIENT MID-PROJECT	STUDIO SPACE DOUBLED BY BREAKING THROUGH WALL

Favorite quotes:

Design that lacks ideas and depends entirely on form for its realization may possess a certain kind of mysterious charm; at the same time it may be uncommunicative.
    Henry James, The Art of Fiction, 1941

One hundred tellings are not as good as one seeing
    Chinese Proverb

AGE. *14 - 41*

STEVE TOLLESON JOB HISTORY [B. 11/1/58]

14

MOVED TO VAIL COLORADO   MOVED TO CHICO   MOVED TO SAN FRANCISCO

73

LAWN BOY SACTO, CA | SHOE DYER DYE PUMPS FOR BRIDESMAIDS | FOOD PREP, CHEF SACRAMENTO, CA | SKI SHOP SALES GUY VAIL, CO. | AUDIO-VIDEO DELIVERY GUY CHICO STATE | WORKED FOR M.A. STUDIO PALO ALTO, CA

> LEARNED FUNDAMENTALS OF SERVICE INDUSTRY   > CRITICAL COLOR MATCHING   > LEARNED VALUABLE PRODUCTION SKILLS   > LEARNED BASICS OF SELF-PROMOTION SALES AND MARKETING   > LEARNED TO DRIVE GO-KART   > LEARNED TO PULL ALL-NIGHTERS

< B.D. A.D. >

There are particular aspects about design that I really enjoy. At the most
general level, I like the purity of design and its use of scale and composition.
I truly enjoy color for its ability to add nuance through subtleties, contrasts
and texture. When we are on press, I love working with the printer to tweak
the details in the ink blends to obtain the most desirable effects. There is
also a great deal of pleasure for me in using different materials – from paper
to plastics to metal – to blend and combine for design effects that solve
communication objectives. Typography is a special passion; and I value it
in all forms – from classic to nontraditional typefaces. For me, all of these
are tools of expression that draw on my roots in fine arts.

I also enjoy the personal interaction that takes place among my co-workers,
myself, and clients. In particular, I've been fortunate to work with an enormous diversity of people, companies, and subjects over the years. What is
especially gratifying is the education process that comes with every design
project. We constantly have to dive into new subjects that we have to grasp
before we begin the design phase. So we are always reading and talking
with clients about almost anything you can imagine – from a sophisticated
hardware or software technology, retail trends, food packaging, sports
equipment, biotechnology, finance, to paper manufacturing.

CAREER PHASE
2

| 1995 | 1996 | 1997 | 1998 | 1999 |

OND TAX AUDIT   THIRD TAX AUDIT   TEN EMPLOYEES   FOURTH TAX AUDIT

Inspiration also comes from keeping a balance between work and family,
no matter what the weekly demand is for scheduling projects, travel, or
deadlines. Outside the studio, I both play and coach basketball and soccer.
I snowboard, and in the past taught for five years at California College of
Arts and Crafts. I believe design plays an important role in business communications, and that it has meaningful impact, but these other activities help
me keep my work in perspective.

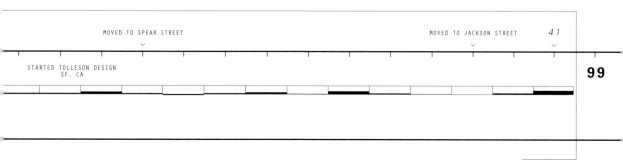

MOVED TO SPEAR STREET   MOVED TO JACKSON STREET   41

STARTED TOLLESON DESIGN
        SF, CA

THE BUSINESS

I don't ever make the mistake of imagining that my design ideas are more valuable than anyone else's. Clients appreciate being treated as sophisticated thinkers who want something unique.

I still can't say no to a new project, even if we're really busy. It's just that every project feels like an opportunity; every project has so much potential and is so interesting.
I always think "how can I say no to learning something new?"

I get a completely different kind of satisfaction from working on web or interactive projects. I have always loved the planning stages of a project. Not just the conceptual planning, but the logistics, the content organization, even the production planning. Interactive projects require so many different considerations, and everything can be determined by each end-user's path.

At any given time, the types of projects on the job list can range from identity to new
product development, from packaging to web sites and may come to us from clients in
industries as diverse as retail clothing, Silicon Valley manufacturing, or genetic engineering.

Since its inception, my studio has grown at a good pace. We established relationships with many of the high-technology businesses of Silicon Valley, which dominated my client list and portfolio at first. Back then I was not concerned about my studio becoming a niche-oriented firm that specializes in one industry or one design category. But after about the third year, encouraged by the momentum of my initial work, I had the opportunity to work on other projects, expanding the portfolio and breadth of work without making project budgets the deciding factor.

THE BUSINESS

From a business standpoint, it has been strategically important to pursue a diversity of work. Solving problems for a wide range of clients, industries, audiences, and media, we accumulate different experiences allowing us to cross-pollinate our thinking for other business projects. Diversity keeps all of us in the studio suitably stimulated.

It's true that my clients are very sophisticated. But I think every potential client is. There is so much great design out there these days: the things we buy, the places we eat, the interiors we live in or shop in or do business in. Every day it is possible to see something we've never seen before which is beautifully designed.

As a result, we have been able to participate in both domestic and international projects, ranging from the interactive to new product development, investor relations and entertainment. We always hear comments from prospective clients about the range of our projects and the lack of a signature look. This is important to me. Each design project needs a completely unique solution, in which we never presume any solution for any client or industry.

Through the years, I've noticed that scale is an important consideration for managing the quality of our work. Maintaining a balance between the office size and the number of projects we take on has a direct bearing on enjoying our work and the ability to remain involved in all the details throughout a project. It also makes it possible to service every client account at the level of commitment I want. No matter what the client asks for, I am completely focused on getting the end result. So I stay very involved throughout every project down to the last detail. Becoming a larger studio would make that involvement impossible.

Whether something is well designed because it's a clever functional design or you have a completely subjective aesthetic response, it is always apparent when the thing started with a clear design intention.

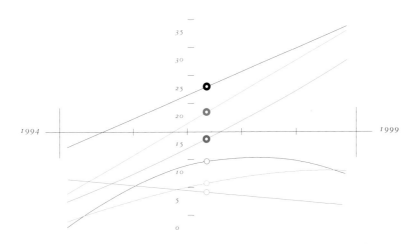

CHANGES IN WORK BY CATEGORY
PROJECTS PER YEAR

◉ identity / branding

◉ product development / packaging

◯ ar / other financial materials

● marketing collateral

◯ interactive / web

◯ interior / exhibit

During the course of 16 years in business, the mix of projects on the job list has swung from one extreme to another — and back again. Long-term client relationships have developed into broad-based collateral programs, web work or even new identities when initially the request was to simply design that year's annual report. While we all have our favorite assignments, the diversity of the work is a part of what we find most interesting.

THE STUDIO ENVIRONMENT

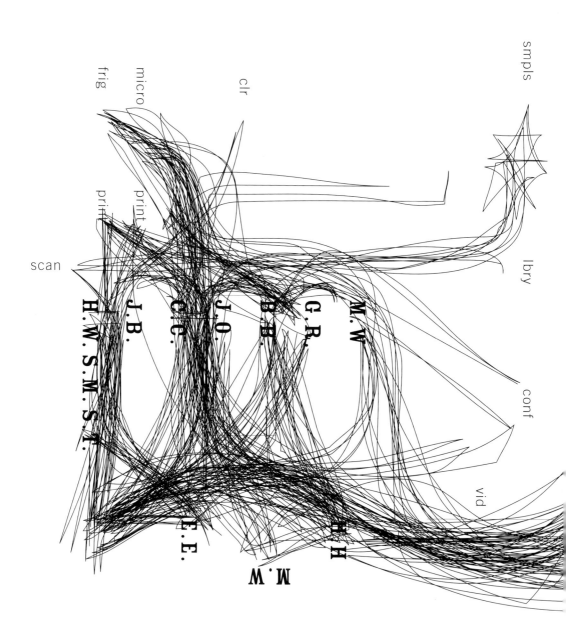

smpls

lbry

conf

vid

frig

micro

clr

print

print

scan

H.W.S.M.S.T.

J.B.

C.C.

J.O.

B.B.

G.R.

M.W

H.H

M.W

E.E.

We work in a stressful industry. There is a lot of pressure to produce creative work under deadlines. Long hours mean we often spend more time with each other than with our families. It only makes sense to make our work space into a place as comfortable and appealing as home, where we feel supported during the most demanding times. This leads to our collective vision that an office should be open, interesting, fun, collaborative, and supportive.

I think the office must be open not only in its floorplan, but also in its lack of hierarchy and professional competitiveness. Everyone who walks in is valued as an individual, personally and professionally. Consequently, I've tried to assemble my studio staff as if I were selecting a family — with an eye to assuring that we all have a personal connection. There's a lot of support in that, as we've seen each other through sick relatives and pet tragedies as well as weddings and band performances. From a design perspective, the open atmosphere is unique. No one worries about ownership, we all contribute freely during reviews and critiques, and when we sit down to conduct a design presentation, it is our collective work.

Just as we pursue a wide range of projects, we also strive to attract and keep a diversity of talented individuals who bring much more than just design credentials to the studio. I've always believed that you don't hire the portfolio as much as you respond to who the person is — which is often of more interest than pure talent alone. As a result, our people are as eclectic as our portfolio.

The studio is a fun place to work. We're not overly concerned with restrictive rules, so we are all more comfortable, a condition I think fosters creativity. Some of my colleagues compare working here to living in a dorm again, or at least like gaining an extended group of siblings. This leads to a positive form of competition during creative brainstorming sessions, when we sit around a table attempting to play off and outdo one another, not only in the quality ideas but the size of the laughs. We also believe in recesses (code: "There's a meeting in the hall!"), and regularly find time to indulge in our favorite network game, Marathon. We compete against one another, have tournaments, keep score, and there is always trash talk going on. It is a great way to relieve stress.

8 hours of [office] traffic. Design is not a static process — it is decidedly kinetic.

STARBUCKS

MOLINARI'S

YANK SING

HOTALING

YO-YO'S

CLOWN ALLEY

SAFEWAY

SPECIALITY

CAMPO SANTO

the place next to the salad place

M

T

W

T

F

We take our food seriously.

●	MARY
◉	HOLLY
◉	SARA
◉	MARK
○	STEVE
○	GABRIELLA
○	BILL
○	JEAN
○	CRAIG
○	JOHN
○	HELENA
○	SHONA
○	ELLEN
○	RENE

 jack in the box

BASIL LEAF

TACO BELL

ORALE-ORALE

BISTRO BURGER

METRO DOG

tricolore
massimo's

GATEWAY TO HELL
House of Nanking

PM

MACARTHUR'S PARK

THE STUDIO ENVIRONMENT

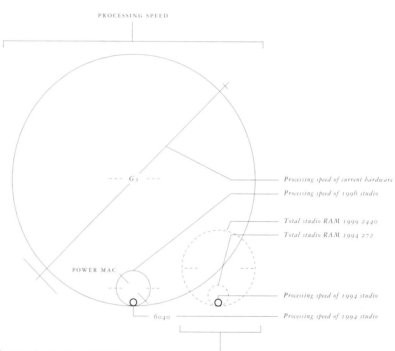

PROCESSING SPEED

G3

Processing speed of current hardware

Processing speed of 1996 studio

Total studio RAM 1999 2440

Total studio RAM 1994 272

POWER MAC

Processing speed of 1994 studio

6040

Processing speed of 1994 studio

MEMORY

As the years advance, so has the muscle required to process our digital files. From floppy disks to Syquest drives to hot-swapping external gigs, we seem to stay just ahead of the curve when it comes to current computer technology. Some old friends linger on in the studio, though. A recently retired IIci, which of late had been relegated to accounting and office managerial tasks, once handled complex design files in its early days — back in 1991. Most recently, a new force of speedy blue G3s has begun to slowly populate the office.

Retail clients inspire another kind of playful phenomenon, in which some people in the office become rabid advocates of a particular client's product. Styles and trends roar through the office with fashion clients. Food clients are even better. That is, except for the microwave popcorn incident which brought seven fire trucks to the street outside the studio.

Given the studio's relatively small size, we accomplish a considerable amount of work. In part, I think it results from the ethic of collaboration we encourage – both with the client and among ourselves. We want clients to be a part of the planning process, because we think it gets us all closer to a real solution. Clients help inform our creative ideas, improving our understanding of their business, and together help create an appropriate solution. The same happens internally. In the studio, we bring a lot of talent together in a group effort. Once someone initiates an idea, it accumulates other designers' input, and we all end up contributing as we refine the concept.

A supportive office environment is the single most important aspect in the studio to ensure we do good work. Fostering that environment has always depended on having what I can only term as healthy, mutually respectful relationships among everyone here. I am committed to making the environment as easy and stress free as possible.

When evaluating a new business opportunity, I typically sit down with everyone and poll our interest in working on it. I also make it a point to keep current with the designers about their preferred work categories, so that I can respond with that type of new business development - be it books or interactive, music or the sports industry. If there are new technology tools involved, as in Web site development, we acquire them and give the designer the time to become proficient in the technology's use. Staying in touch with my colleagues' personal interests and ventures is an important part of what makes our office work.

Chronology of Marathon names in the studio:

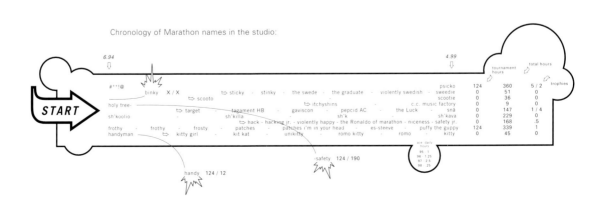

soak wash rinse spin

360 STUDIO VIEW

crit wall

libra

kitchen

bill's area

conference room

mark's area

mary's, holly's, ellen's area

old wall

sarah's area

front door

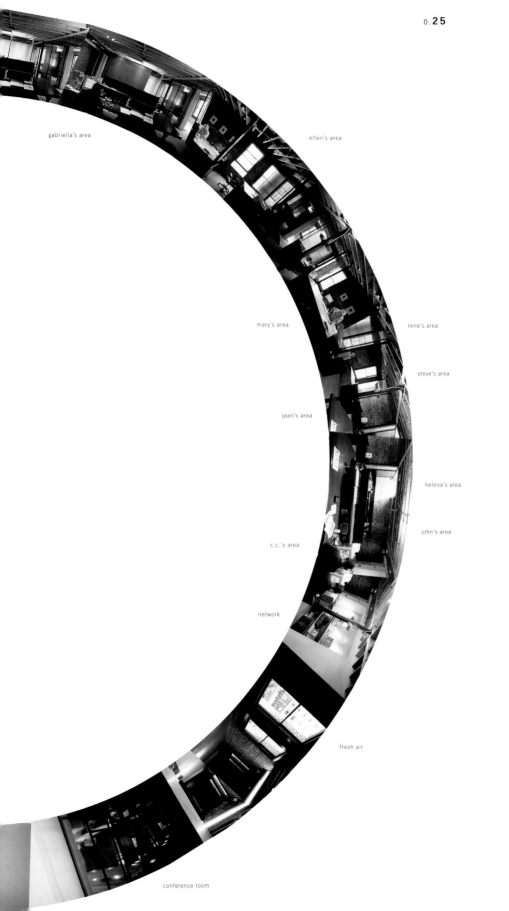

gabriella's area

ellen's area

mary's area

rene's area

steve's area

jean's area

helena's area

john's area

c.c.'s area

network

fresh air

conference room

SK	WSH
INSERT CARD	ENTER PIN
DEPOSIT COIN	LISTEN FOR DIAL TONE
COMMAND	OPTION
LIFT/CLOSE LID	SIT/STAND
PUSH IN CLUTCH	TURN OVER ENGINE
AWAKE	EAT
REMOVE FROM CARTON	PULL STRING
ADD GRINDS	ADD WATER

RNS	SPN
COMPLETE TRANSACTION	TAKE CASH/RECEIPT?
DIAL NUMBER	SPEAK
SHIFT	ESCAPE
RELEASE	FLUSH
SHIFT INTO FIRST	RELEASE CLUTCH/DEPRESS GAS
WORK	SLEEP
EXPOSE ADHESIVE	APPLY TO CUT
TURN ON	SIP

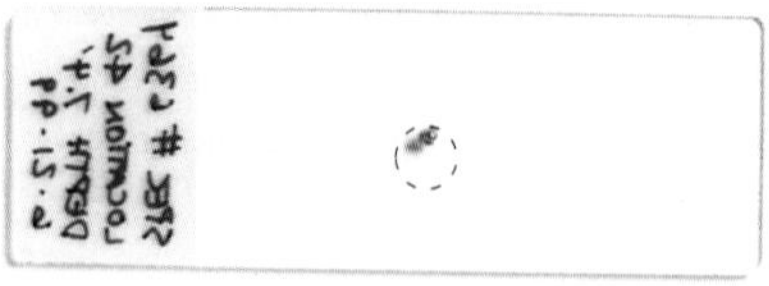

SLIDE # 63rd
LOCATION G45
DEPTH 14'
PP .15 .9
P .15 .9

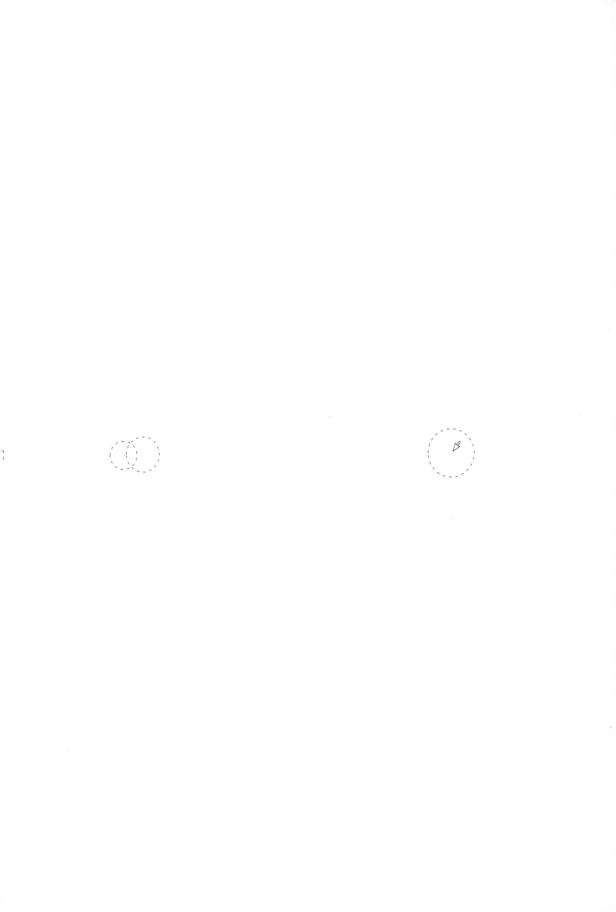

CLIENT: RPI   PROJECT: Post-graduate program series

PUBLICATION
p1-INFORMATICS p2-INTELLIGENT WORKPLACE   1997

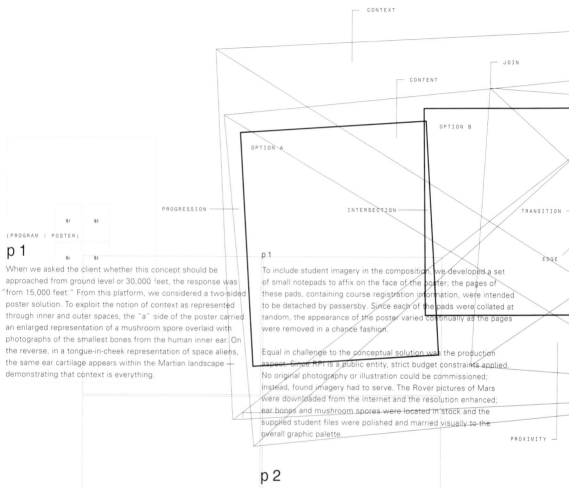

CONTEXT

JOIN

CONTENT

OPTION B

OPTION A

PROGRESSION   INTERSECTION   TRANSITION

Q1   Q2

(PROGRAM / POSTER)

p 1

Q4   Q3

EDGE

When we asked the client whether this concept should be approached from ground level or 30,000 feet, the response was "from 15,000 feet." From this platform, we considered a two-sided poster solution. To exploit the notion of context as represented through inner and outer spaces, the "a" side of the poster carried an enlarged representation of a mushroom spore overlaid with photographs of the smallest bones from the human inner ear. On the reverse, in a tongue-in-cheek representation of space aliens, the same ear cartilage appears within the Martian landscape — demonstrating that context is everything.

p 1

To include student imagery in the composition, we developed a set of small notepads to affix on the face of the poster; the pages of these pads, containing course registration information, were intended to be detached by passersby. Since each of the pads were collated at random, the appearance of the poster varied continually as the pages were removed in a chance fashion.

Equal in challenge to the conceptual solution was the production aspect. Since RPI is a public entity, strict budget constraints applied. No original photography or illustration could be commissioned; instead, found imagery had to serve. The Rover pictures of Mars were downloaded from the internet and the resolution enhanced; ear bones and mushroom spores were located in stock and the supplied student files were polished and married visually to the overall graphic palette.

PROXIMITY

p 2

A second commission from RPI came to us in the form of the Intelligent Workstation, otherwise known as "The Future of the Future is in the Present." This course of study focused on the shifting paradigms and new possibilities for the spaces we occupy to do "work." The "intelligence" in the workplace refers to a building's ability to meet changing environmental, business and human needs; in other words, the use of artificial intelligence to create smart structures.

To promote this course offering, side #1 of the poster displays a menu board from a restaurant (the type you might find sitting outside on the sidewalk) advertising "Today's Specials." These specials are not of the edible variety, but are instead the elements of a typical work environment:
Monday's Special: Fluorescent lighting
Tuesday's Special: Music
Wednesday's Special: Air conditioning

On the verso of the sheet, a placemat (complete with doodles) illustrates course options and contact information. As an alternative, we suggested a lazy Susan — associated with each condiment on the wheel were the various components of the course structure and other relevant details.

ENVIRONMENTAL
OPTION MENU
LIGHT
SOUND
HEAT
NOISE

SPACE

Designing the call to action for the Informatics and Architecture program at Rensselaer Polytechnic Institute began with our own education into the school's philosophy and direction. Informatics is defined as a program of study "in designed ambiguity where technology and design are to be considered as components of a radical rethinking of a new architectural practice." Steeped in the belief that the practice of architecture, while reliant upon computational precision, is an explicitly imprecise science, the program proposes to develop and encourage appropriate sensibilities about technology and its role in design.

TRANSFORMATION

GROUPING

BOUNDARY

PUBLICATION
p1 -INFORMATICS POSTER   1997

Mars
ˇ

affiliation
ˇ

title
ˇ

DIR N°   1 . 0 - FRONT

CLIENT   RPI   PROJECT   program information

ARCHITECTURE RENSSELAER

Informatics and Architecture

* * *

where   a program in designed ambiguity (1)
are to be considered as   technology and design (2)
of   components of a radical rethinking (3)
                 architectural practice (4)

(1) It is essential to maintain an operative ambiguity when working with the precision of computational tools in the design profession. We believe that architectural design is explicitly not a precise practice, and it is a severe mistake to reduce it to this based on the tools employed. We are continually looking at ways to broaden the scope of computational tools, using their precision where useful, and new means of employing them where not. (2) This program is about neither design nor technology as autonomous disciplines. All work–theoretical and applied –is about both, and how each can inform the other. (3) We are not interested in producing technophiles, we are interested in developing sensibilities about

technology and on the conceptualization of its role in one´s methods of design; at the same time, however, we are immersing ourselves in technology. It is an experiment at best: to reconsider that which has been called revolutionary requires intensive immersion. (4) The proposition that architecture is somehow inarticulated through built form is simply no longer appropriate. The means of addressing the design of space of human habitat, have expanded vastly in this century and no longer defer to the 'art of building.' The technologies under consideration explicitly facilitate a consideration of how entertainment, communication, and mass media have begun to effect our spatial perceptions.

1, 2, 3, 4,   see above

Take me to your leader.

Q1   Q2

course descriptions

graduate seminar

Taught collaboratively with our other post-professional graduate programs, Smart Architecture and The Intelligent Workplace, this seminar will serve as the core for discussion and critique of student and faculty projects.

environment 1
⌄

degree courses
⌄

dingbats

Graduate Academic and Enrollment Services
Rensselaer Polytechnic Institute
110 8th street
Troy, NY 12180

be brought together and discussed on a semi-regular schedule via this course. These studios are expected to be design and research based, with an intensive focus on experimental methods. It is the less formal counterpart to the graduate seminar course.

concentration electives

Students will need to plan a course of study with their academic advisor between the time of their acceptance and introduction into the program and the first day of classes. These four electives (16 credits) are expected to develop a rigorous introduction to the students' field of research. These courses are to be taken from architecture rensselaer's graduate course offerings and from the diverse offerings available throughout the institute.

Q3

Q4

contact information

Graduate Academic and Enrollment Services
Rensselaer Polytechnic Institute
110 8th street
Troy, NY 12180

email: information.architecture@rpi.edu
www.rpi.edu/dept/arch/IA
application material and info: 518.276.6789
email: grad.service@rpi.edu
www.rpi.edu/Departments/admissions/

ARCHITECTURE RENSSELAER

D

04

03

01

Informatics and Architecture

ARCHITECTURE RENSSELAER

R P I

I

ARCHITECTURE RENSSELAER

IA is an integrated two-year design study and laboratory program organized for the theoretical and practical reconsideration of the role of technology in the design of architecture, urbanism, and life. The School of Architecture at Rensselaer Polytechnic Institute is offering this program to architectural practitioners, graduating students from any profession, and post-graduates in architecture who are sharing a thoughtful technological reconsideration of their skills.

A new program at this time, IA intends to become a leader in international research initiatives on technology-based design.

Providing a strong foundation in both theory and practice, degrees in IA will prepare students with professional backgrounds for advancement in both academic research and professional developments. Graduates will have developed an informed and critical knowledge of the latest software and hardware tools which exist in the workplace, and will be empowered to advance themselves and their profession together. The IA program offers both a post-professional Masters of Architecture or a Masters of Science, both in Informatics and Architecture, to assist both in architectural professionals interested in advanced explorations of computer technology in their practice and in technologists interested in the role technologies play in the design of their architectural surroundings.

In your year, students will be able choose from 3D-animation, computer-aided manufacture, virtual reality design, graphics programming, and video editing software programs to study and apply to unfinished research projects. Architecture Rensselaer currently teaches Softimage 3D, Form-Z, and Infini-D for modeling and animation, Microstation for CAD, WorldUp and WorldToolKit for virtual reality design and programming, and Softimage/Eddie for video editing. In addition, courses on a multitude of programming languages exist throughout the curriculum. These technologies will serve as the foundation for software development, experimentation, and design integration that will become a integral part of the IA program, as well as for the theoretical research which is already a strength of the school. All software is available and taught in labs, in the school's new remotely, a Silicon Graphics hardware based advanced visualization and simulation lab for high-end graphics design work and work of the using graphic workstation labs around the Institute's campus. Our faculty are both knowledgeable on the intersections of technology in design technique and adept at understanding their more conceptual role in the field of architectural design and research.

The program is designed to support a network of professionals who cannot come into a similar year design program as well as academics who want a focused time to perform research. Courses span two successful academic terms (a fall and spring term), and the research project is encouraged to extend into a third term. This additional term should encourage the incorporation of the research program into the student's professional and extra curricular interests. In addition, summer continuing education courses on software interaction are offered for those who would like to get an advanced introduction to our technologies.

environment 2
∨

eardrum
∨

PUBLICATION
p1 - INFORMATICS POSTER

CLIENT: RPI

PROJECT: program information

DIR. N°   1.0 - BACK

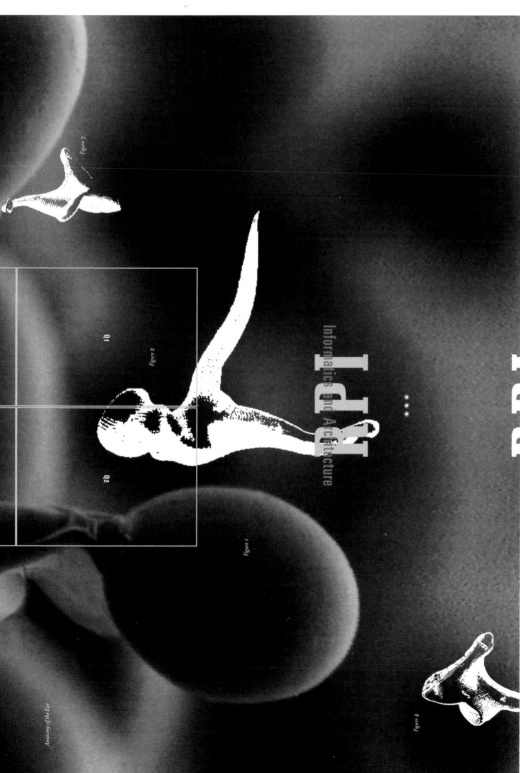

Figure 3

Figure 2

01

02

Informatics and Architecture

RPI

Figure 1

Anatomy of the Ear

Figure 4

PUBLICATION
p2 -INTELLIGENT WORKPLACE 1997

INTRO

TITLE

2.0 · FRONT

DIR N°

PROJECT: program information

CLIENT: RPI

N° 1

menu

The Intelligent Workplace

RESEARCH DESIGN LEADERSHIP

Open 24 hours, 7 days a week

RENSSELAER POLYTECHNIC INSTITUTE

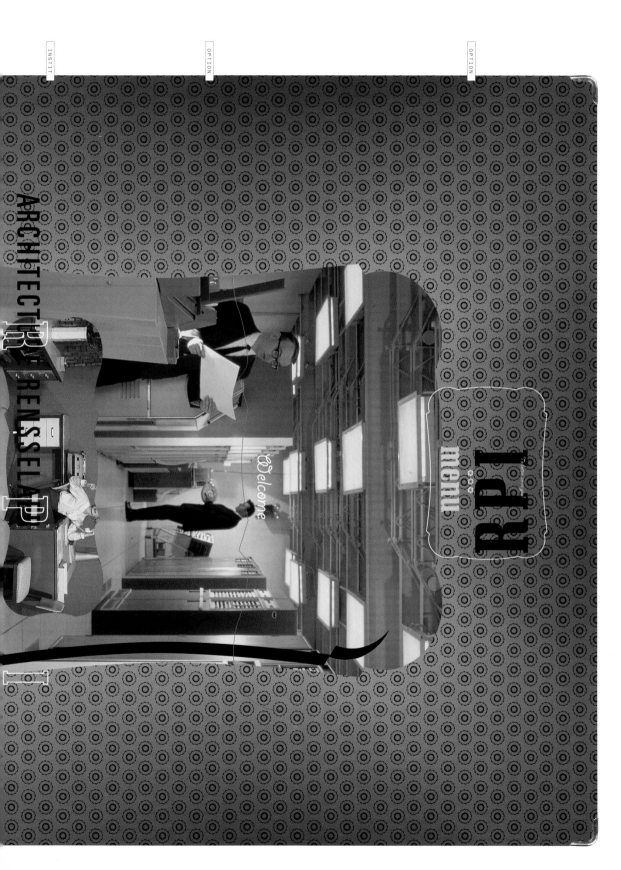

INSTIT OPTION OPTION

ARCHITECTURE RENSSELAER P

Welcome

menu

RPI

SPECIAL
ALT.
OPTION
INTRO
CHOICE
OPTION

ARCHITECTURE RENSSELAER

RENSSELAER POLYTECHNIC INSTITUTE

The meaning of work is being redefined through emerging technologies, video-conferencing, long-distance learning, advanced communication and information systems, changes in management strategies, and globalization. Concerns about productivity raise important issues related to the physical and environmental aspects of the workplace. Smart materials and technologies and artificial intelligence offer opportunities to transform the quality of the workplace. These developments along with new forms of organizational and facility management strategies, create the need for intelligent workplace models. The need for effective, healthy, sustainable, responsive and intelligent workplaces covers many building types (e.g. offices, factories, laboratories, schools) and are needed throughout the world.

Program Objectives This graduate study program exposes students to new perspectives and possibilities to prepare them for leadership roles in architecture, building science and facility management. Its radical approach to interdisciplinary study in a technological context helps participants understand the nature of emerging technologies and the design of intelligent workplaces within the context of intelligent buildings. The emphasis is on the research, design, and performance of intelligent workplaces. Of particular interest is the impact of intelligent workplaces on architecture, building economics, facility management and productivity.

The Program Rensselaer's School of Architecture graduate study program. The Intelligent Workplace leads to a Master of Architecture post-professional degree, or a Master of Science in Building Sciences degree. The Program is conducted within the setting of a research design laboratory in an integrated architecture and technological environment. The Program offers students the opportunity to gain extensive knowledge in emerging technologies, material concepts and emphasizes the unique challenges and opportunities of designing tomorrow's intelligent engineering, and architectural environment as work. The impact of intelligent workplace technologies on worker... research/design project. Within the context of one of the world's leading technological universities ... ...master's thesis in the final semester of study.

SPECIALS

Daily specials served daily. No substitutions please
Specials are served from 11:30 am–3:30 pm

Monday
This would be copy briefly explaining a customized
combination available this day.

Large Video Confer   Small Video Seminar
Demo Theater   Gaming   Distance Learning Center

Tuesday
This would be copy briefly explaining a customized
combination available this day.

Telebooth   Light-Shower Room
Acoustic Vibration Chairs @ Silent Sounds

Wednesday
This would be copy briefly explaining a customized
combination available this day.

Large Video Confer   Small Video Seminar
Demo Theater   Gaming   Distance Learning Center

Thursday
This would be copy briefly explaining a customized
combination available this day.

Telebooth   Light-Shower Room
Acoustic Vibration Chairs @ Silent Sounds

Friday
This would be copy briefly explaining a customized
combination available this day.

Large Video Confer   Small Video Seminar
Demo Theater   Gaming   Distance Learning Center

SIDES

Choose two (2) of any of the following to accompany
your main selection.

Thermal Comfort
Daylight
Sound Surround
Noise Suppression
Fresh Air
Illumination Level
Humidity Control
Color Renditions
Shading Control
Visual Privacy Curtain

PUBLICATION
p2 - INTELLIGENT WORKPLACE POSTER   1997

CLIENT: RPI   PROJECT: program information   DIR N°   2.0 - BACK

SIDE

MENU

FEATURE

menu

The Intelligent Workplace

RESEARCH · DESIGN · LEADERSHIP

Open 24 hours, 7 days a week

Intelligent Workplaces

Designed, integrated, and managed to meet changing environmental, business and human needs.

The intelligent workplace includes equipment, furnishings, space and enclosures whose integrated systems are capable of anticipating and responding to internal and external phenomena that effect the performance of the building and its occupants.

The intelligent workplace creates an environment through which organizations achieve their business or manufacturing objectives and enhance the productivity and creative potential of its occupants while allowing efficient management of resources with minimum life-cycle costs.

Select the spaces and places you need today and reserve them for tomorrow!

SELECTIONS

The selections found below come accompanied with your choice of two (2) of the side orders.

Think Capsules
This would be copy briefly explaining the idea behind this room and its potential contents.

Telebooth ◇ Light-Shower Room
Acoustic Vibration Chairs ◇ Silent Sounds

Productivity Game Rooms
This would be copy briefly explaining the idea behind this room and its potential contents.

Large Video Confer. ◇ Small Video Seminar
Demo Theater ◇ Gaming ◇ Distance Learning Center

Team Work Rooms
This would be copy briefly explaining the idea behind this room and its potential contents.

Pillows, Darts and Boards ◇ Everything + Kitchen
Escape From Reality ◇ Virtual Reality ◇ Sound Surround

Entrees

School of Architecture
Rensselaer Polytechnic Institute
Troy, NY 12180-3590

phone (518) 276-6978
fax (518) 276-3034
http://www.rpi.edu

Think Capsules
This would be copy briefly explaining the idea behind this room and its potential contents.

Telebooth ◇ Light-Shower Room
Acoustic Vibration Chairs ◇ Silent Sounds

Productivity Game Rooms
This would be copy briefly explaining the idea behind this room and its potential contents.

Large Video Confer. ◇ Small Video Seminar
Demo Theater ◇ Gaming ◇ Distance Learning Center

Team Work Rooms
This would be copy briefly explaining the idea behind this room and its potential contents.

Pillows, Darts and Boards ◇ Everything + Kitchen
Escape From Reality ◇ Virtual Reality ◇ Sound Surround

In the Fall of 1998, Liz Claiborne invited Tolleson Design to its corporate headquarters in New York. With this visit, we found ourselves embarking on an exploration of attitudes toward the existing corporate brand identity, possible new directions, and a total immersion into the world of retail fashion. We were invited to quiz a broad range of employees at various functionary levels for insights into their vision for the company. Their unanimous goal, we learned, was to revitalize the brand and to generate awareness through a new symbol and its applications.

NEW SYMBOL HERE

z claiborne

We came away from these conversations with a series of recurring attributes — the Liz Claiborne brand was consistently perceived as modern, feminine, aspirational, American, functional, classic. We heard the same things from nearly everyone — they all felt the need to strengthen the Liz Claiborne brand, that it made sense to capitalize on the equity existing in the name and to eliminate any distractions in terms of unnecessary elements in order to arrive at a singular notion.

We took them at their word — literally — and structured a visual exploration of icons that reflected the characteristics they had identified. We wanted to include the whole company in our process so we presented nearly all of the hundreds of iterations we produced as our thinking about the brand and symbol evolved.

CLIENT: Liz Claiborne   PROJECT: id / applications

APPLICATIONS
SYMBOL APPLICATIONS   **1999**

As we immersed ourselves in the Liz Claiborne culture, we became educated not only about the company, its long history and many sub-brands, but also about the market, the industry, and the competition. Our study of the research findings identified the age and background of a typical customer. This profile was enlightening and startling:

While the contemporary woman is aware of the impossibility of all the roles she is asked to play — mother, wife, professional, family banker/accountant, housekeeper, cook — she also believes she has no choice. Given the diversity of her many roles, she no longer has the opportunity to "change costumes" between scenes. As a result, her clothing is no longer a form of self-expression but an exercise in functionality and appropriateness. While dressing more casually than before, the contemporary woman defines this casualization in terms of versatility — not necessarily as sloppy or less "dressy" — reflecting the blurring of boundaries between her public, professional, and private life. Dressing comfortably and appropriately are no longer mutually exclusive.

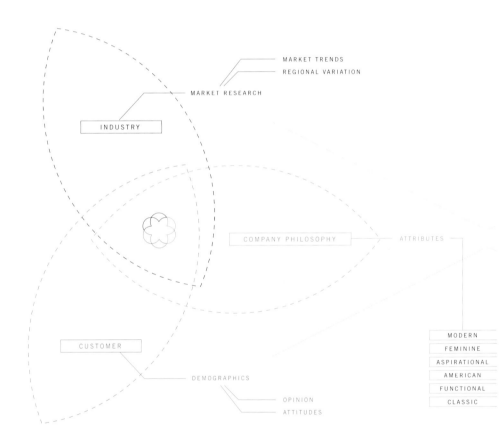

We also learned that there are three major influences to the Liz Claiborne brand — the overall industry or market, the customer demographic, and the company's philosophy and heritage. From our understanding of these components, we distilled the six key attributes that formed the basis of our search for the new identity.

In speaking with our contacts, reading the available studies and researching the industry, we developed our own impressions of the past, present and future of the Liz Claiborne brand. We came to understand what was liked and what wasn't working. After listening to all of this input, we compiled and distilled the things we heard into the outline of possible directions. Out of the key attributes associated with the Liz Claiborne brand came long lists of associative words, each one adding another piece to the picture as we sought to redefine the essence of the Liz Claiborne identity.

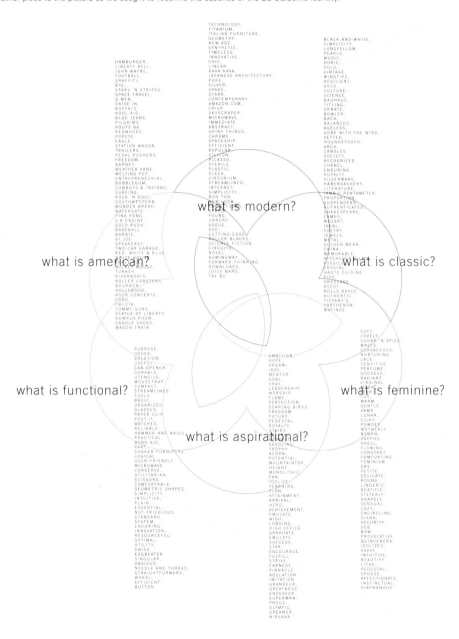

A logo associated with the Liz Claiborne brand in the recent past assumed a triangular form. Some opinions held that the triangle was passé, too strongly associated with our mothers' generation; others thought it might have some value and might be revived. The triangles that we developed have been updated, reinvented, finessed. We looked at flowers and flames, spirals and gems, squares and circles and lines, stars and stripes. The selections that follow include some of what we contrived. We then culled our picks and rendered them in a range of sizes and in color.

APPLICATIONS
SYMBOL APPLICATIONS

The symbol is suggestive of a host of complementary imagery. The sculptural quality of the outer form belies the solidity of its geometry. The outer shape is stable, the inner triangle is in motion. The symbol is imbued with a sense of both softness and strength; it is grounded and energetic. It exudes a powerful presence while connoting something more expressive. Not exactly a study in contradictions, the mark instead suggests a marriage of extremes. Something old, yet something new.

The symbol was built to function at all sizes, in every conceivable situation. The simplicity of the execution allows the mark to be transformed elegantly to accommodate a range of executions — the outer shape is stable, unmoving; the inner form pivots ever so slightly on its axis to allow it to scale perfectly.

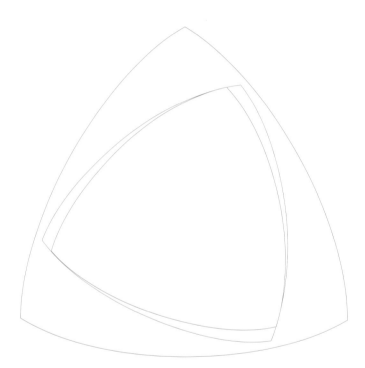

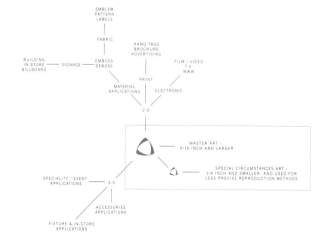

color exploration　　　　deboss sample

tissue paper　　　　　final color palette

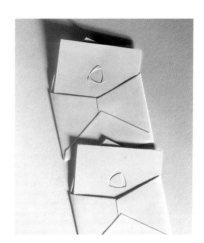

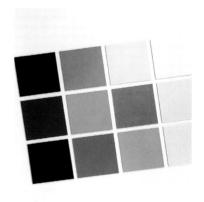

In bringing this symbol to life, we were chartered to create a palette of applications demonstrating the mark's versatility. The more we've worked with the mark, the more we like it. It continually suggests to us additional avenues for interpretation. No matter the choice of color, material or pattern, the expression assumes a secondary position to the impact made by the brand. The new symbol definitely has its own personality.

The test of any logo is in its most simple form — black and white. And while we've adorned the symbol with a variety of color combinations and presented it in a variety of media, we are still drawn back to the simplest version. In this form there is no embellishment; there are no frills — this mark has nothing to hide.

CLIENT: Liz Claiborne   PROJECT: id / applications

APPLICATIONS
SYMBOL APPLICATIONS   1999

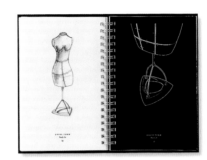

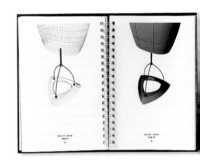

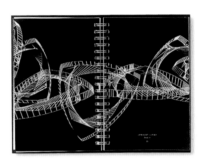

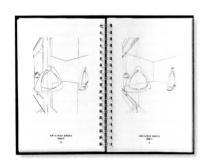

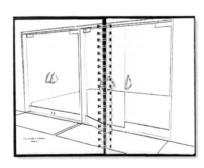

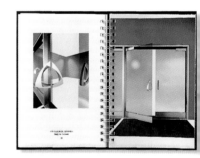

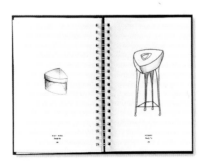

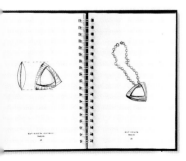 

As the development of the brand continues, we have continued to explore and anticipate other categories for application. Extending the symbol into an array of two- and three-dimensional objects — everything from jewelry to handbags, perfume bottles to tea sets — has demonstrated the versatility and extensibility of the new image.

We have taken a flight of fancy or two and compiled the results from these journeys into a series of small booklets. Such forays into product, accessory, and fixture development extend the influence of the brand far beyond its print application.

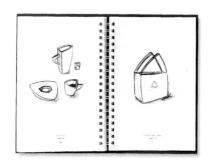 

CLIENT: Liz Claiborne   PROJECT: id / applications

APPLICATIONS
SYMBOL APPLICATIONS   1999

woven labels   paperclips

bottle stopper   garment hangtags

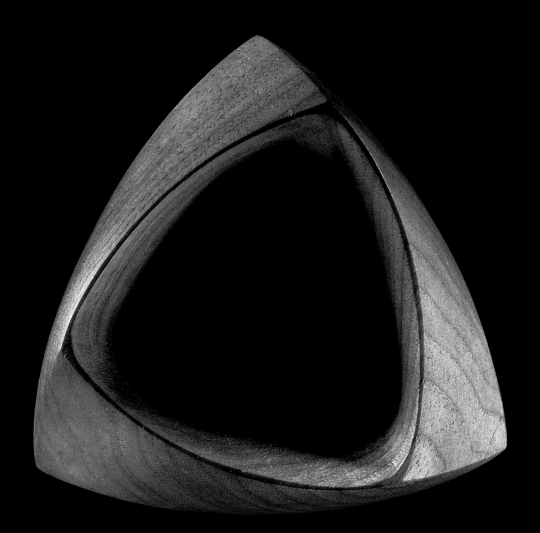

walnut bangle   perfume bottle

CLIENT: Zap Me! PROJECT: id / product development

APPLICATION
PRODUCT DEVELOPMENT AND PROTOTYPE   1997

```
SPACE
  ↓
WWW
  ↓
ZAP ME! PROTECTED WWW
  ↓
ZAP ME! CONTENT    ]──→  DEMO
  ↓                        ↓
INDIVIDUAL SCHOOL
  ↓                        ↓
USER        ←─[    DEMO AUDIENCE
```

A.0 NEWSSTAND Z-NEWS
A.1 CURRENT EVENTS
A.2 MAGAZINES
A.3 STUDENT NEWS
A.4 TEACHER NEWS
A.1.1
A.2.2

B.0 WHAT'S NEW/Z-APP'NING
B.1 NEW PLACES
B.2 STUDENTS
B.3 TEACHERS

C.0 REFERENCE/Z-SOURCE
C.1 MUSEUMS
C.2 TOOLBOX
C.3 DICTIONARIES
C.4 ATLAS
C.5 LIBRARY
C.1.2 LOUVRE
C.1.3 SMITHSONIAN

D.0 SAFETY/Z-SAFETY
D.1 DEPT. OF HEALTH
D.2 EMERGENCY
D.3 AAA

E.0 GAMES/Z-ZONE
E.1 STUDENT
E.2 NEIGHBORHOOD
E.3 CHAT
E.4 MOVIES
E.5 MUSIC
E.6 GAMES

F.0 BEST OF ZAP
F.1 STUDENTS
F.2 TEACHERS
F.3 LEADERSHIP PROGRAM

G.0 CURRICULUM/Z-CLASS
G.1 SCIENCE
G.2 THE ARTS
G.3 MATH
G.4 SOCIAL SCIENCE
G.1.1 ASTRONOMY
G.1.2
G.1.3

H.0 CAREER GUIDANCE/Z-FUTURE
H.1 COMPANIES
H.1 COLLEGES
H.1 US FORCES
H.1.1 JOB SEARCH

I.0 OUR SCHOOLS/Z-SCHOOL
I.1 FEATURED
I.2 WEB SITES

J.0 TEACHER'S LOUNGE/Z-STORE
J.1 SPECIAL CURRICULUM
J.1 LESSON PLANS

Satellite On-Line Solutions came to Tolleson Design with a request to design the identity and, ultimately, an interactive demo for a new product, Zap Me!. Zap Me! was to be a broadcast product, synthesized from content beamed via satellite from educational, local community and strictly limited, on-line sources to corporate-sponsored workstations located in schools and libraries. As the product at this stage was still an idea, the logical first step was to establish the site content for the demo. Then we would determine the identity, site navigation plan and develop the interface that would support it.

PROTOYPE FUNCTIONALITY LEGEND

 FULL GRAPHIC   TEMPLATE   LINK   DEFINITELY   POSSIBLY   ANIMATION   SOUND   VIDEO S

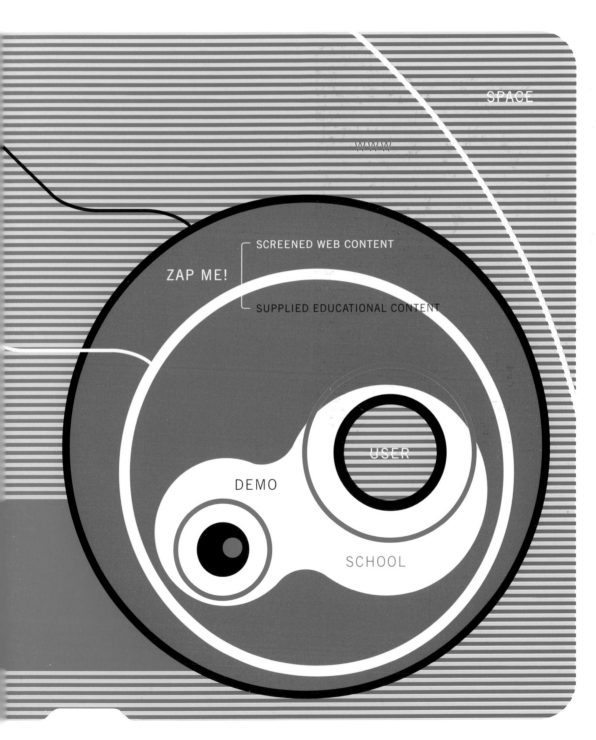

SPACE

W.W.W

ZAP ME!

SCREENED WEB CONTENT

SUPPLIED EDUCATIONAL CONTENT

USER

DEMO

SCHOOL

Zap Me! space is a protected area buffered from direct interaction with the worldwide web. It is a self-contained entity — an environment within an environment. Only filtered content reaches the end user.

N° 3

CLIENT: Zap Me!　　　PROJECT: id / product development

APPLICATION
BRANDING AND IDENTITY TEST　　　1997

A

A.1

A.2

A.3

The requirements for the Zap Me! symbol were that it be fun and active; it should also appeal to an audience ranging in age from grade K through 12, spanning diverse cultural, economic and ethnic backgrounds. Once we had created a series of Zap Me! icons, they were tested by kids, in three groups: K through age 6, ages 7–9 and 10–12. The solution that had the highest rating was then carried forward into the identity applications and the interface design.

B

B.1

B.2

B.3

C

C.1

C.2

C.3

CLIENT: **Zap Me!**   PROJECT: id / product development

APPLICATION
BRANDING AND IDENTITY TEST   **1997**

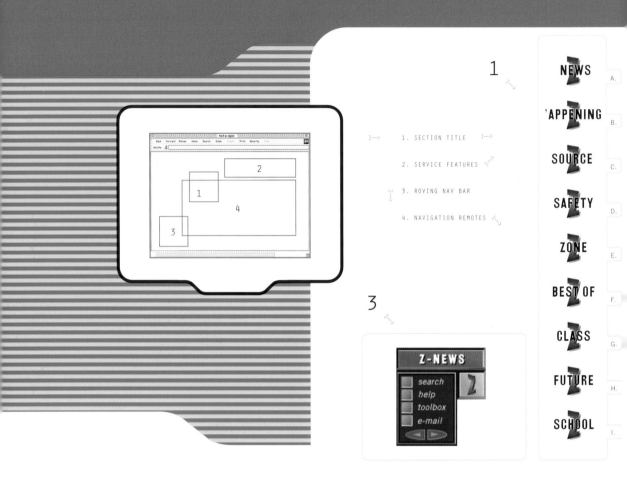

1

1. SECTION TITLE

2. SERVICE FEATURES

3. ROVING NAV BAR

4. NAVIGATION REMOTES

NEWS — A.
'APPENING — B.
SOURCE — C.
SAFETY — D.
ZONE — E.
BEST OF — F.
CLASS — G.
FUTURE — H.
SCHOOL — I.

3

Z-NEWS
search
help
toolbox
e-mail

We implemened the selected mark as a series of buttons and icons facilitating interactive navigation. The interface had the additional requirement that it should relate visually to current gaming technology which would be a familiar metaphor for the target audience. The interface features a tear-off menu that travels with the students wherever they surf the internet. It can be used to access other Zap Me! resources or simply to return home (e.g.: to school). The navigation system is composed of a series of animated spinning, bulging, bouncing windows, and was designed to visually reference remote control devices.

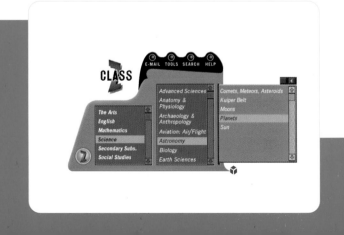

2

IT SPINS!

IT BULGES!

LOUNGE

RELATED

SEEK

HOME

SEARCH

TOOLS

E-MAIL

HELP

4

SOURCE

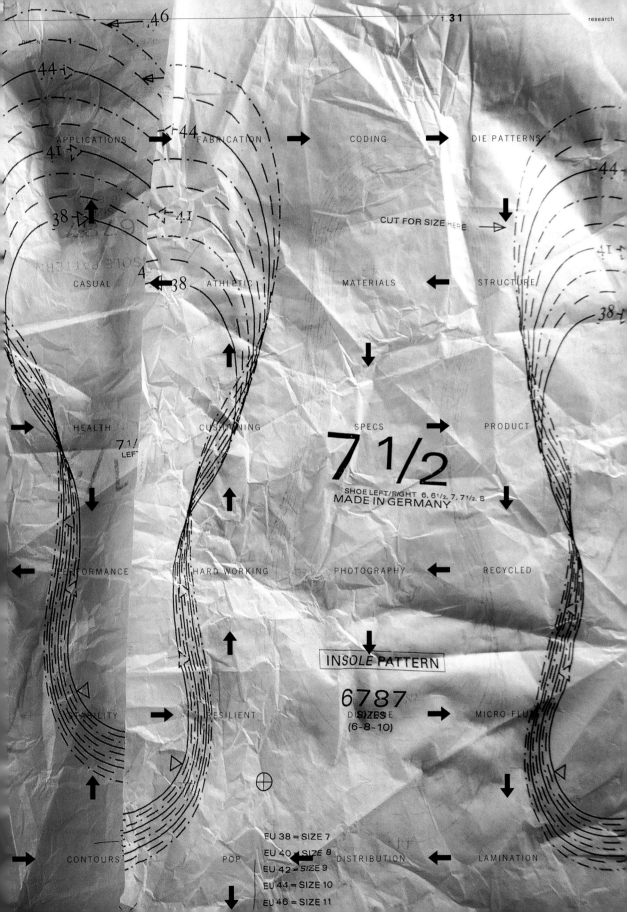

The process diagram on the previous page overlays the tissue wrapping used to package the insoles. It outlines the path we followed to learn the Birkenstock philosophy, devise the product strategy and ultimately produce the insole packaging.

Birkenstock, widely known in the U.S. since the 1950s for its distinctive footprint sandals, decided to introduce their shoe inserts into the domestic market in the fall of 1995. For a company founded on the belief that foot health is the basis for overall well-being, they felt they could most effectively spread their philosophy by retrofitting shoes of other manufacturers to their model of comfort and stability.

BIRKENSTOCK

Since competition for recognition in the retail environment is keen and insoles don't command the attention from the sales force that fashionable shoes are afforded, the packaging and display solutions created for Birkenstock inserts had to sell the product on their own. Hence the decision to depict a range of lifestyle situations on the fixtures and boxes, to associate a contemporary color palette to the various styles and to provide a "touch me" cut-out so the customer could feel the quality of the materials that composed the insoles. These packages eventually were translated and offered for sale in several European countries. The claim that Birkenstocks represent "German engineering for your feet" aptly describes the degree of care and attention devoted to the manufacture of their product. Below are final studies for Birkenstock insole packaging.

TOLLESON DESIGN wash rinse spin

CLIENT: Chronicle Books   PROJECT: commemorative book

PUBLICATION
GI JOE: THE STORY OF A MAN OF ACTION   1997

ALPHA   BRAVO   CHARLIE

RECON

3 RETREAT/REGROUP
What size is the book? Restructure the entire 200+ pp. book based on new size. *But wait! Initial size was correct!* Re-restructure the entire 200+ pp. book based on original size.

1 INITIAL OBJECTIVE
Capt. M. Winn decides to lay the book out in PageMaker. Attempts to lead Quark coup. Leaves for Europe.

BATTLEFIELD

MAJ. W.J. BOWERS

CAPT. M. WINN

2 MAIN ASSAULT
Maj. W.J. Bowers leads next assault. Restructures from PageMaker back to Quark. Troops assembled by Pvt. R. Rosso. Weekend attacks break down vital links.

HDQTRS

PVT. R. ROSSO

GEN. S. TOLLESON

4 INFILTRATION
General Tolleson planning daily strategies and inspiring mission strategies. Giving W.J. Bowers feedback for next Recon.

5 REVIEW CYCLES
Daily visual reviews in question. Bringing to light all substantial and interesting anomalies.

ECHO   **FOXTROT**   **GOLF**

SITTING AROUND THE WAR ROOM. REMEMBERING BATTLES WON AND LOST IN OUR OWN BACKYARDS. THE DAYS FROM OUR CHILDHOOD WHERE WE USED TO DESTROY, MANGLE, AND ABUSE OUR WAR TOYS. BRINGING INSPIRATION TO THE BOOK—THESE EVENTS WERE ALL SO VIVIDLY EMBEDDED IN OUR MEMORIES. AND HOW AMAZINGLY FAMILIAR SOME OF THE STORIES WERE. HERE ARE A FEW OF THOSE SUCH EVENTS. AND IF YOU DECIDE TO TRY SOME OF THEM, FOLLOWING.THE RECOMMENDED PARTICIPANT LIST ENSURES YOUR ENJOYMENT OF SUCH ACTIVITIES.

1-3 PARTICIPANTS:

We used to shave his head and put a match or lighter to his face until he'd start to melt, transforming him into a post-nuclear war victim or mongoloid Joe and head, melting him, giving him a big chin and deformed features.

3-5 PARTICIPANTS:

We'd tape pieces of plastic straw to Joe's hands and then thread about thirty feet of string through it. Someone [Person A] would get on top of the house or climb a tree with one end of the string and Joe. Someone else [Person B] would hold the other end of the string down on the ground some distance away. The third person [Person C] would station himself some distance away from the string, poised with a BB gun. Person A would let go of Joe, sliding him down the string. Person C would take aim at the moving target. Hitting Joe would send him spinning the rest of the way down.

2-4 PARTICIPANTS:

We'd tie all of our Joes to a G.I. Joe Army Jeep. Joes all piled on together, hanging off the sides, we'd tie the jeep to our bikes and ride around the neighborhood. Joes flying all over the place. Our dad got out his Super8 and got the action on film. Tight shot on the jeep barreling through the neighborhood looked pretty real.

1-2 PARTICIPANTS:

An M-80 and Joe is a vast and open arena nurturing an array of creatively destructive possibilities.

1-2 PARTICIPANTS:

A effective means at antagonizing younger kin: Find a willing Barbie Doll. Strip both G.I. Joe and Barbie down to their bare plastic bodies. Dress Joe, as best you can, with Barbie's attire and place the action figure in an obvious location that will allow your younger sibling to easily find it.

INCOMING MESSAGE > > > > >

WHEN CHRONICLE BOOKS AND HASBRO JOINED FORCES

WAR ROOM

INFO.CENTER.

CLIENT: Chronicle Books   PROJECT: commemorative book

PUBLICATION
GI JOE: THE STORY OF A MAN OF ACTION   1997

3/4"

TO PRODUCE A RETROSPECTIVE OF GI JOE'S 35 YEARS OF NEIGHBORHOOD ENGAGEMENTS, OUR INTERNAL RESEARCH MACHINE WENT INTO OVERDRIVE. EACH AFTERNOON, BILLY'S BATTA

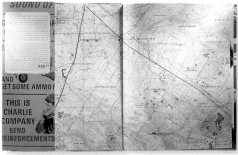

NAME: DATE: /   /

1000 FT.

1/2"

G I

...UP IN THEIR BUNKER, ARE SIEGED BY MARK'S MARAUDERS FROM THE OTHER SIDE OF THE DESKTOP. "LEADING THE CHARGE, JOE RACES HEADLONG TOWARD THE ABYSS AT THE FAR END OF

TOLLESON DESIGN wash rinse spin

Nº 5

CLIENT: Chronicle Books   PROJECT: commemorative book

PUBLICATION
GI JOE: THE STORY OF A MAN OF ACTION   1997

1500 FT.

G.I. JOE® SAYS

5/8 "

THE TABLE THEN PLUNGES HEADLONG TO THE FLOOR AS SHOUTS AND CHEERS ECHO THROUGH THE HALLS. BACKYARD RECOLLECTIONS ARE THE ORDER OF THE DAY—STORIES OF PURSUITS

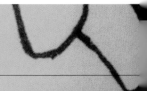

N LANDSCAPES ARE RECOUNTED OVER AND OVER. A COMIC BOOK ENERGY PERVADES THE ENVIRONMENT AS EVER MORE INCREDIBLE ACCOUNTS OF THE INCARNATIONS OF JOE ARE RELIVED.

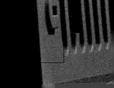

CLIENT: Microsoft   PROJECT: id, interface

PUBLICATION
ENCARTA 2000 IDENTITY AND INTERFACE   1997

When Microsoft set out to redefine its online encyclopedia, Encarta, for the year 2000 release, one important parameter was for the product's identity to extend not only to the icons that facilitate navigation through the encyclopedia, but even to the interface and organizational system of the software. Our challenge was to influence functionality through design. We began by assimilating the body of information that Microsoft had already compiled about the future product's content and function.

INFLUENCE PRODUCT INTERFACE
ASSOCIATION TO ORGANIZATION
/ NAVIGATION
DEFINE PATHS
DETERMINE GRAPHICAL LANGUAGE
DEFINE PRODUCT PARAMETERS
AFFECT PRODUCT USE
DETERMINE APPROACH TO CONTENT

MAP SUBJECT ASSOCIATIONS
AFFECT CONTENT NAVIGATION
DETERMINE ACCESS PATHS
RESEARCH LINKED SUBJECT AREAS

INFLUENCE PRODUCT
INTERFACE

REFER TO MASSIVE
CONTENT ARCHIVE

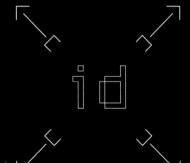

INFLUENCE PRODUCT
NAVIGATION

ASSOCIATION TO INTERFACE
/ ORGANIZATION
ESTABLISH USER/CONTENT RELATIONSHIP
SUGGEST SYSTEM FOR
RELATIONAL INFORMATION ACCESS
DETERMINE INFORMATION RETRIEVAL

INFLUENCE PRODUCT
CONTENT ORGANIZATION

ASSOCIATION TO INTERFACE /
NAVIGATION
DEFINE INFORMATION HIERARCHY
SUGGEST LINKING STRUCTURE
ALLOW FOR RANDOM ACCESS

Several possible scenarios emerged from this assignment. In one version, an ever-present character acts as a guide to lead the user through the maze of data; alternately, the user could employ a magnification device to aid in looking ever deeper into the heart of the information. In other versions, the user is a traveler faced with branching paths as he embarks on a quest for knowledge, or clusters of content mimic an astronomer's map of the galaxies and stars.

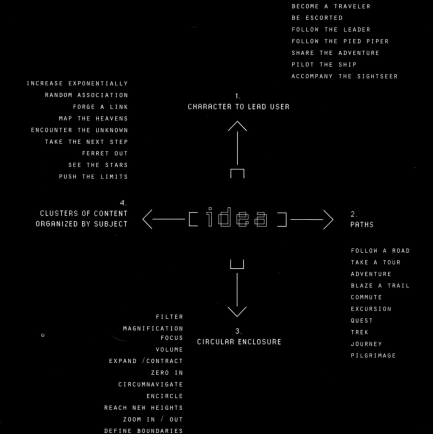

SERVE AS A GUIDE
BECOME A TRAVELER
BE ESCORTED
FOLLOW THE LEADER
FOLLOW THE PIED PIPER
SHARE THE ADVENTURE
PILOT THE SHIP
ACCOMPANY THE SIGHTSEER

INCREASE EXPONENTIALLY
RANDOM ASSOCIATION
FORGE A LINK
MAP THE HEAVENS
ENCOUNTER THE UNKNOWN
TAKE THE NEXT STEP
FERRET OUT
SEE THE STARS
PUSH THE LIMITS

1.
CHARACTER TO LEAD USER

4.
CLUSTERS OF CONTENT
ORGANIZED BY SUBJECT

idea

2.
PATHS

FOLLOW A ROAD
TAKE A TOUR
ADVENTURE
BLAZE A TRAIL
COMMUTE
EXCURSION
QUEST
TREK
JOURNEY
PILGRIMAGE

FILTER
MAGNIFICATION
FOCUS
VOLUME
EXPAND /CONTRACT
ZERO IN
CIRCUMNAVIGATE
ENCIRCLE
REACH NEW HEIGHTS
ZOOM IN / OUT
DEFINE BOUNDARIES
DIG DEEPER
ROTATE
CIRCULATE
SURROUND
ENCOMPASS

3.
CIRCULAR ENCLOSURE

PUBLICATION
2000 ENCARTA CONCEPT BOOKS   1997

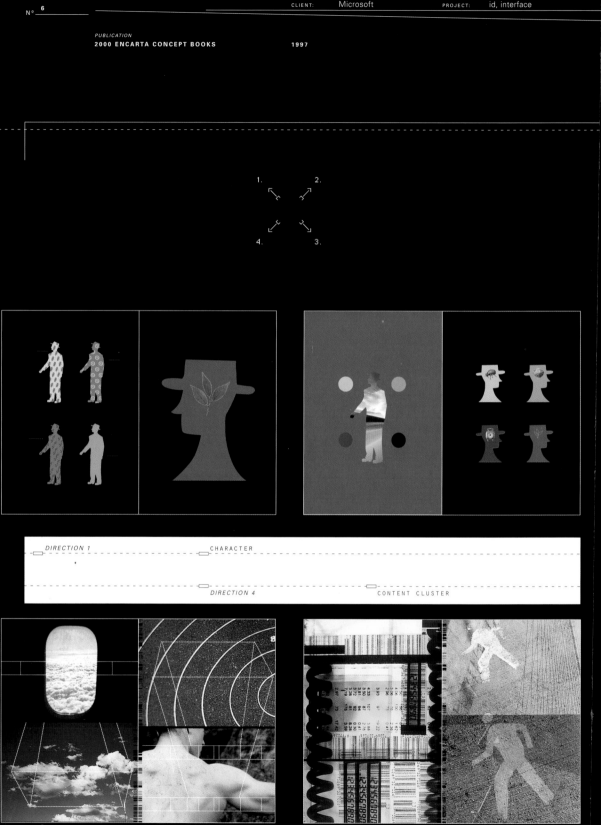

1.   2.

4.   3.

DIRECTION 1   CHARACTER

DIRECTION 4   CONTENT CLUSTER

Once our thinking was in place, we presented the concepts in the form of 4 books. The albums are assembled as workbooks containing the visual exploration and support for our ideas. Their purpose is to explain, to elaborate on the point of view we are attempting to convey. The images they contain begin to confer visual form onto the concepts

DIRECTION 2   PATHS

DIRECTION 3   CIRCULAR ENCLOSURE

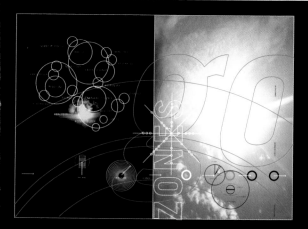

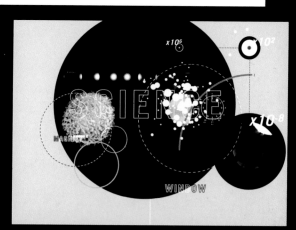

N° 6

CLIENT: Microsoft   PROJECT: id, interface

PUBLICATION
CONCEPT VISUALIZATION   1997

ROAD	CONDUIT	SEEK
HIGHWAY	PLAN	PURSUE
TRACK	METHOD	EXAMINE
TRAIL	MODE	HUNT
PASSAGEWAY	CAREER	INQUIRE
BYWAY	SCHEME	ASK
SHORT CUT	POLICY	RESEARCH
ALLEY	DEVICE	PROBE
LANE	MEANS	QUERY
SIDEWALK	SPHERE	EXPLORE
AVENUE	LOOP	SCOUR
CIRCUIT	PATTERN	CHASE
RUT	GLOBAL	
TRAJECTORY		
ORBIT		
GROOVE		
COURSE		

]---> A]---> B   linear - path /directional focused search

A.1 ———— B A   nonlinear sequential

NAVIGATION AND CONTENT ORGANIZATION SYSTEMS:

A - **Path**, LITERAL

| 1 | 2 | 3 | 4 |...| 0 |

A.1 - Chronological
A.2 - Focused
A.3 - Random

B - **Path**, SYMBOLIC

0101001010110101111
101110101001010100
001010101100110111
0
10
101
00101

B.1 - Global, holistic
B.2 - Infinite
B.3 - Code

C - **Search**, LITERAL

]---> O <---[

C.1 - Sets
C.2 - Hierarchy
C.3 - Perspectives

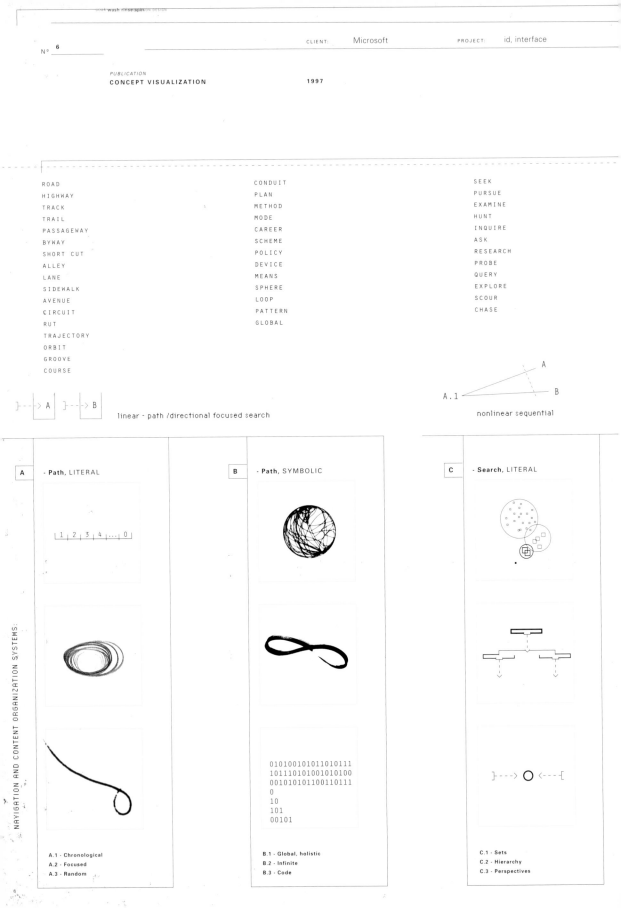

An exploration of words and basic icons was the next step on the path toward a symbol. If we thought anyone in the world would identify any one of these icons with its intended meaning, then, there might be the germ of a symbol in it. From these descriptive concept illustrations we began to distill the ultimate symbol. Since the Encarta identity would encompass an interactive component as well as more traditional applications, this broad-based inquiry held particular merit.

PERSPECTIVE	ACCIDENT	SOLVE A PUZZLE
HIERARCHY	LEARN	CHRISTOPHER COLUMBUS
BURIED TREASURE	ENCOUNTER	BREAK A CODE
BEACON	REVEAL	WITNESS
HOLY GRAIL	UNVEIL	UNEARTH
X MARKS THE SPOT	INVESTIGATE	LIGHT BULB
EINSTEIN	FIND	UNDER THE CARPET
INTUITION	UNCOVER	PRIVATE EYE
WATER-WITCHING	VERIFY	
	ESTABLISH	
	BETRAY	

layered · navigational

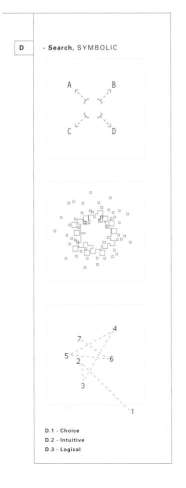

D - Search, SYMBOLIC

D.1 - Choice
D.2 - Intuitive
D.3 - Logical

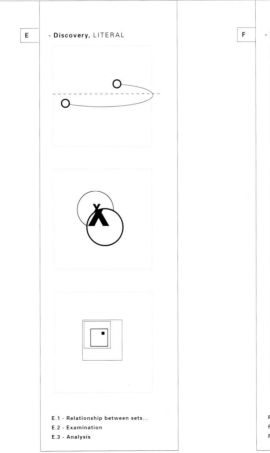

E - Discovery, LITERAL

E.1 - Relationship between sets...
E.2 - Examination
E.3 - Analysis

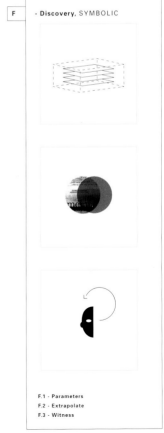

F - Discovery, SYMBOLIC

F.1 - Parameters
F.2 - Extrapolate
F.3 - Witness

The symbol for Encarta evokes overlapping concepts and layers of complexity. The mass of imagery elicits a sense of explosion of information and the excitement of discovery. Alternate treatments represent variations of the symbol, which were developed for different uses.

FINAL ANIMATED SYMBOL USAGE 1-6

ENCARTA

E
Λ

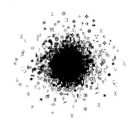

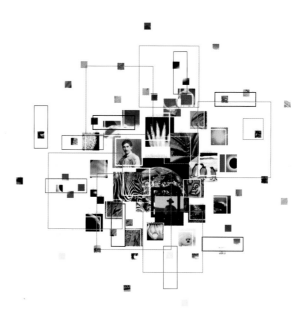

The structure of the logo itself became the organizing principle for the interactive component of the software. Each inquiry reveals another assortment of associations. Zooming in and out to locate different levels of content, drilling down through layers of information, the user animates the static symbol, and summons a whole new set of relationships previously hidden from the foreground.

EX. 1   MEDICINE

HEALTH   DISEASES   EX.: ANXIETY DISORDERS

              FITNESS

PHYSICS

ENERGY

EX. 2   SPACE

SCIENCE   CHEMISTRY

1.0		2.0		3.0		4.0
.1	ASTROPHYSICS	.1	ALTERNATIVE FUEL CELLS	.1	ASTRONAUTS	.1	BIOCHEMISTRY
.2	ATOMIC PHYSICS	.2	BIOMASS	.2	AVIATION AND AEROSPACE MEDICINE	.2	CHEMICAL PHYSICS
.3	BIOPHYSICS	.3	ELECTRICAL POWER	.3	CIVILIAN SPACE TRAVEL	.3	CHEMOMETRICS
.4	CHAOS	.4	ENVIRONMENTAL IMPACT	.4	DEEP SPACE	.4	CHROMATOGRAPHY
.5	CONDENSED MATTER	.5	FUEL CELLS	.5	EXPERIMENTS	.5	COMPUTATIONAL CHEMISTRY
.6	CRYSTALLOGRAPHY	.6	FUSION	.6	EXPLORATION	.6	ELECTROCHEMISTRY
.7	FLUID DYNAMICS	.7	GEOTHERMAL	.7	MICROGRAVITY	.7	MOLE DAY
.8	MECHANICS	.8	HYDROPOWER	.8	REMOTE SENSING	.8	MOLECULAR DATABASE
.9	NUCLEAR PHYSICS	.9	NUCLEAR	.9	SATELLITES	.9	ORGANIC CHEMISTRY
.10	QUANTUM CHEMISTRY	.10	PETROLEUM	.10	SETI	.10	POLYMERS
.11	RELATIVITY	.11	SOLAR POWER	.11	SPACE AGENCIES	.11	SONOCHEMISTRY
.12	SUPERCONDUCTIVITY	.12	SONOLUMINESCENCE	.12	SPACE STATIONS	.12	SPECTROSCOPY
.13	X-RAY			.13	SPACECRAFT		

CLIENT: Electronics for Imaging   PROJECT: annual report

PUBLICATION
EFI ANNUAL REPORT   1997

97

TASK	PHASE 1 - RESEARCH		
WEEK	0	1	2

RESEARCH
CONCEPT
CONTENT

digital color printing

> >   >   >   >

efi technology   new technologies   research production
                                                  applications

efi market position   company message   develop concept
                                                  platforms

client needs   case studies

96

0
1
2
3

[SEE PAGE .0.51 >

4

4

B   G

BLUE = SOOTHING   YELL

COOL PACIFY CONTROLLED TRANQUIL REFRESHING SKY AZURE PRUSSIAN CERULEAN   = W

C

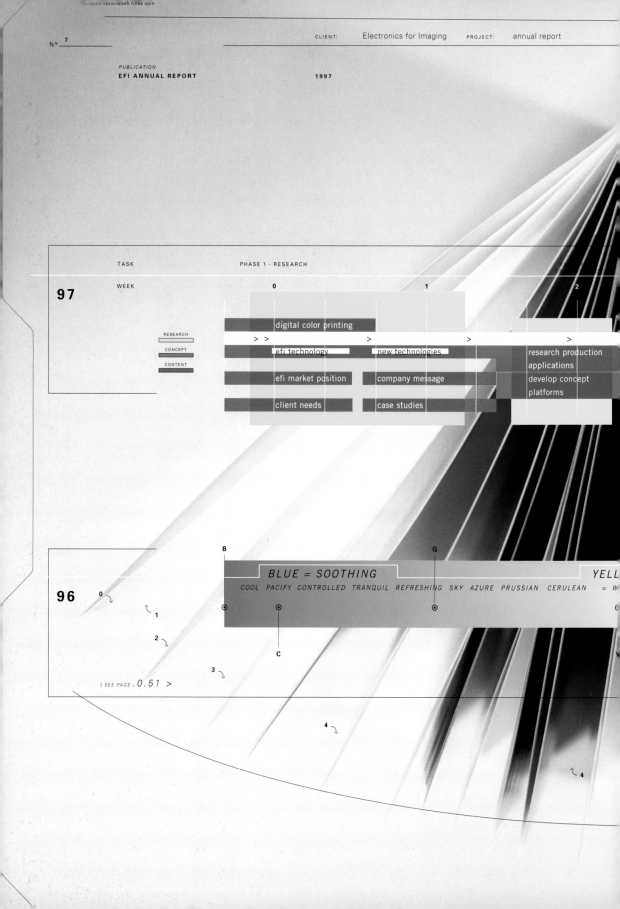

The theme of EFI's 1997 Annual Report, Mission (Im)Possible, is inspired by the many business communication tasks that would have been unthinkable only a short time ago, but which are now routinely achievable because of EFI's Fiery technologies. On-time, high-quality, worldwide distribution of critical documentation — such as this annual report — is a key success factor for supporting any core mission. In the case of this particular annual report, we had the added imperative to research and educate ourselves, then conceive and produce the book using the new EFI technology within a six-week time frame.

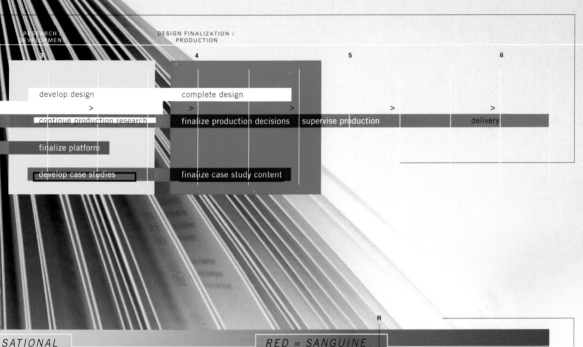

RESEARCH /
DEVELOPMENT

DESIGN FINALIZATION /
PRODUCTION

3	4	5	6
develop design	complete design		
>	>	>	>
continue production research	finalize production decisions	supervise production	delivery
finalize platform			
develop case studies	finalize case study content		

SATIONAL

RED = SANGUINE

GLOWING BRIGHT BUTTER SENSATIONAL = PASSIONATE HOT FLAMING ROSY SIZZLING SOCIALIST CARDINAL COMMUNIST

R

M

THE COLORISTS MANIFESTO [SEE PAGE 0.55 - 0.57 >

There are two kinds of change. The first is incremental, a slow, methodical evolution of events. The second is revolutionary, a dramatic breakthrough with such impact on the status quo that things never seem the same from that point forward. The force of EFI's color revolution is the ease and quality with which the world is able to print out digital documents. Whether it's running a high-speed digital press or hosting web-based, on-demand printing, the Fiery server can be a desktop printer or a production speed copier. It can be across the room or around the world. The color revolution means that you can print what you want, where you want, when you want it.

The 1997 company message is representative of the broad range of digital formats achievable through Fiery technology. Folded into successively smaller posters and attached inside the annual report, the placard starts at a convenient letter size, then opens to reveal pages of tabloid, double-page and parent sheet dimensions — all achievable through Fiery printing. Color dominates each face of the pull-out, opening with a subdued grey-scale introduction, moving through cool shades (blue pages calmly announce the year's earnings as the green tabloid delivers the president's revolutionary message) to the company's branding philosophy, depicted against a radiant golden background, finally reaching a crescendo as the product family is revealed in Fiery red hues — at the heart of the revolution.

PUBLICATION
EFI ANNUAL REPORT   1997

0

ELECTRONICS FOR IMAGING, INC.
1997 Annual Report

1

NOTES

From: "EFI Finance" <finance@efi.co
To: <electronics for imaging shareh
Subject: Re: Notes to Consolidated
Date: Tues, 31 Mar 1998 14:04:44 -0

NOTES TO CONSOLIDATED FINANC

Note 1: The Company and Its Signifi

The Company and Its Business
Electronics for Imaging, Inc. (the
that enable high-quality color prin
hardware and software technologies
ufacturers into fast, high-quality
technologies to increase the output
printers. The Company operates in o
ment manufacturers in North America
to date has resulted from the sale

Summary of Significant Accounting P
Basis of Presentation   The accompa
the Company and its subsidiaries. A
eliminated in consolidation.

The preparation of consolidated fin
ing principles requires management
amounts of assets and liabilities a
of the consolidated financial state
reporting period. Actual results co

Revenue Recognition   Revenue is re
obligations remain and collectibili
potential sales returns are recorde

Cash, Cash Equivalents and Short-Ter
deposits with major banks, money mar
The Company is exposed to credit ri
issuers of these investments to the

The Company has classified its inve
rities are stated at fair value wit
stockholders' equity. Such unrealize

Cash equivalents consist of short-te
months or less. As of December 31, 1
for-sale securities, of which approx
Approximately $45.7 million had stat
Approximately $39.3 million had stat
the Company had approximately $150.2
mately $10.1 million were classified
maturities greater than one year. No
greater than two years as of Decembe

Concentration of Credit Risk   The C
of its customers to the extent of an
performs ongoing credit evaluations
estimated credit losses, such actual

Fair Value of Financial Instruments
investments, accounts receivable, ac
sented in the financial statements,
and prevailing interest rates.

2

[1-4] From the typewriter type on the onionskin cover to the word-processed table of contents and the dot matrix
shareholder's introduction to the mission statements distributed via e-mail, the typographic styles in this annual
report mirror the not-so-very-lengthy history of print technology. Plastic report covers from the corner copy center are
inserted as dividers overlaying the opening pages of the editorial and financial sections, just as they might appear had
you output your copies at a service bureau after downloading the file off the www.

3

From: "EFI Finance" <finance@efi.com>
To: <electronics for imaging shareholders>
Subject: Selected Consolidated Financial Data
Date: Tues, 31 Mar 1998 14:04:44 -0500

4

To demonstrate how the new EFI technologies highlighted across the pages of the annual report accelerate business communications in new ways, we printed a portion of the run as Fiery Prints. In addition, we posted an electronic version of the annual report to the EFI website, providing their shareholders the option of outputting a Fiery-printed version at their own location, or at any Fiery-equipped copy center. It is our way of illustrating the power and utility of these extraordinary tools to communicate without the conventional limits of time and space.

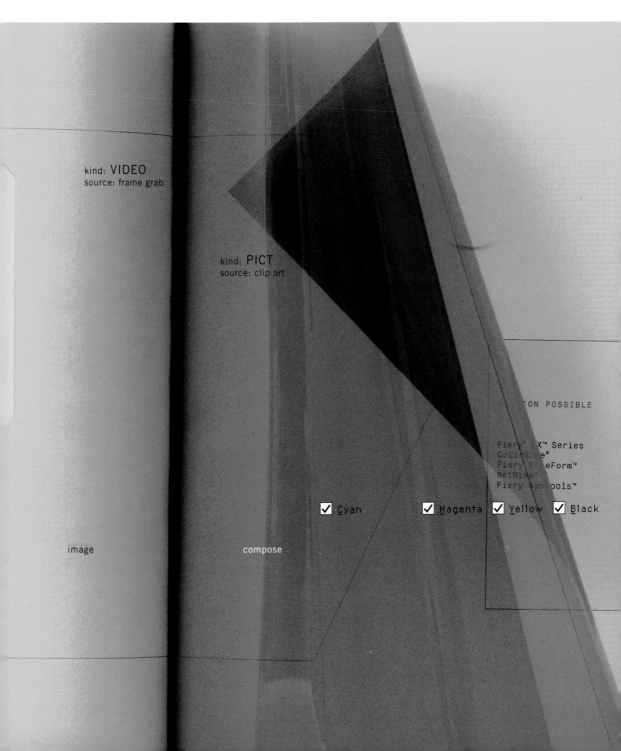

kind: VIDEO
source: frame grab

kind: PICT
source: clip art

...ON POSSIBLE

Fiery X™ Series
ColorWi e®
Fiery F eForm™
NetWi e™
Fiery eb ools™

☑ Cyan   ☑ Magenta ☑ Yellow ☑ Black

image   compose

CLIENT: Electronics for Imaging   PROJECT: annual report

PUBLICATION
EFI ANNUAL REPORT   1997

send

art from marketing dept. / Mac /

financials via FTP / Web /

final documents / ready at 1:30

MISSION: Integrate all final
drafts into one document
Date: Fri, July 17, 1998
To: Sara : John
From: Malcolm : Karl

Subject: Final Business Plan for
Federal Saving and Loan Bank
Message: Incorporate finals from
everyone, we need three perfect
documents for appointment Tuesday
morning at Federal

sales by region / mainframe /

charts from operational / PC /

contribute   **print**

merge

Date: Tues, Feb 15, 1998
To: S. Tolleson
From: A. Borg, Director
Subject: AR
Re: Schedule

Message:
Research new technologies,
demonstrate each in annual,
produce in six weeks including
web version

p 12>13

p 16>17

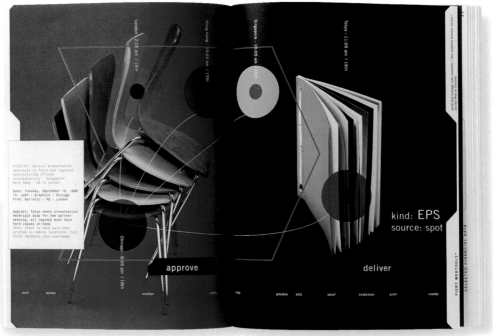

calibrate

London 2:00 am / 19th   Hong Kong 10:05 am / 19th   Singapore 10:05 am / 19th   Tokyo 11:05 am / 19th

MISSION: Deliver presentation
materials to Tokyo and regional
manufacturing offices
simultaneously : Singapore:
Hong Kong : HQ in London

Date: Tuesday, September 15, 1998
To: John / Graphics / Chicago
From: Barretto / HQ / London

Subject: Tokyo needs presentation
materials asap for new partner
meeting, all regions must have
hard copies in-hand
Note: Check to make sure they
printed in remote locations: full
color handouts plus overheads

kind: EPS
source: spot

Chicago 8:05 pm / 18th

approve   **deliver**

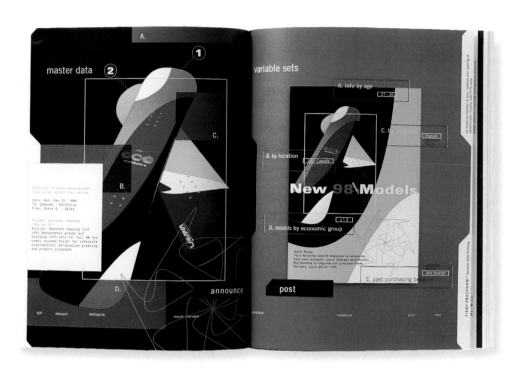

p 14>15

p 20>21

CLIENT: Electronic For Imaging   PROJECT: annual report

PUBLICATION
EFI ANNUAL REPORT   1996

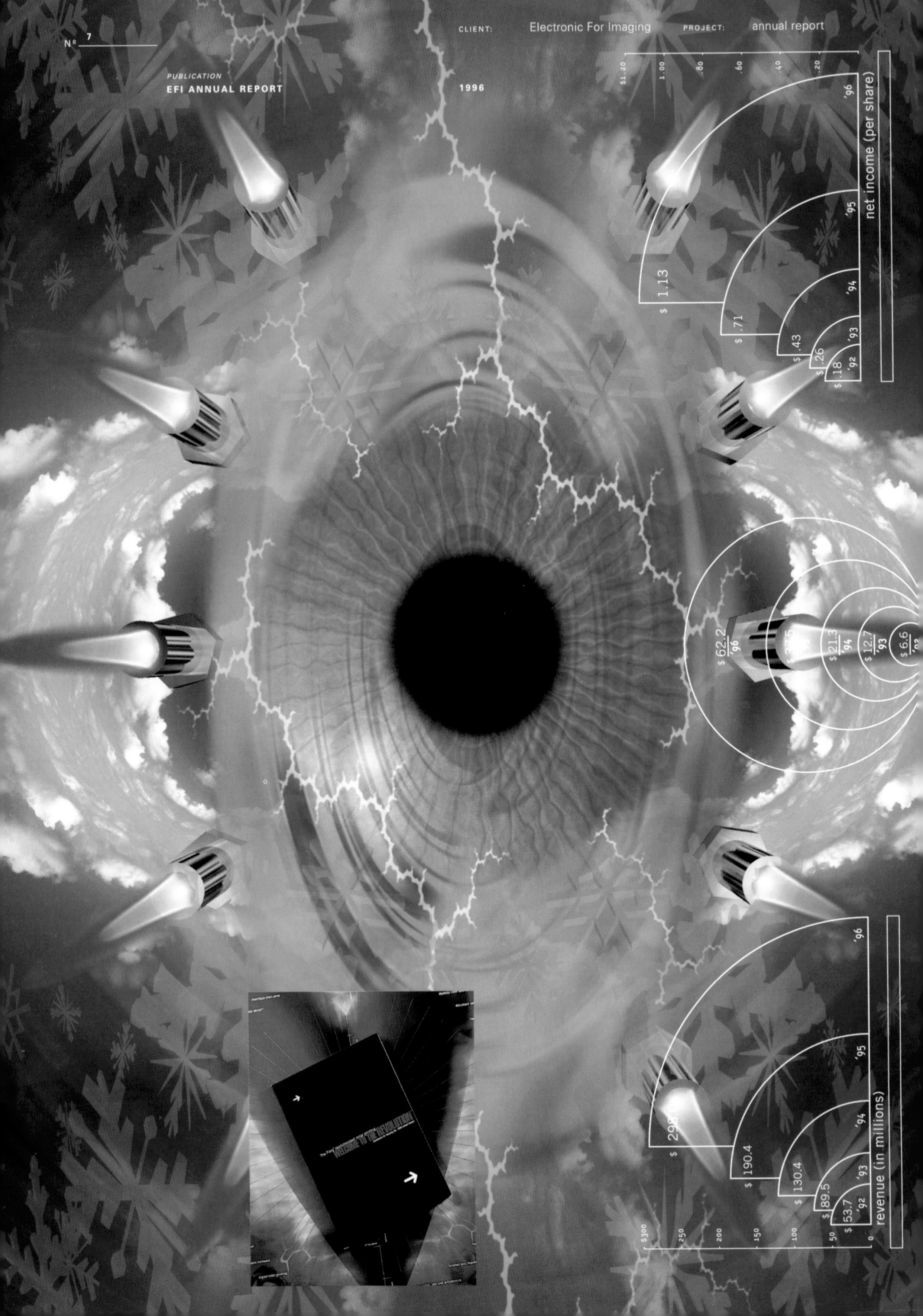

net income (per share)

$1.20   1.00   .80   .60   .40   .20   '96

$ 1.13

'95

$ .71

'94

$ .43

'93
$ .26

'92
$ .18

revenue (in millions)

$ 62.2
'96

$ 21.3
'94

$ 12.7
'93

$ 6.6

'96

'95

$ 298.

$ 190.4

'94

$ 130.4

'93
$ 89.5

'92
$ 53.7

$300   250   200   150   100   50   0

FIERY IS EVERYWHERE

MANIFESTO OF THE COLORIST PARTY

A SPECTRUM IS HAUNTING THE WORLD — THE SPECTRUM OF COLOR. ALL THE POWERS OF THE OLD ORDER HAVE ENTERED INTO A HOLY ALLIANCE TO EXORCISE THIS SPECTRUM: THE COLOR BLIND, THE GRAY SCALERS, THE HALF TONERS, AND THE MOIRE PATTERNS.

WHERE IS THE PARTY IN OPPOSITION THAT HAS NOT BEEN DECRIED AS COLORIST BY ITS OPPONENTS IN POWER? WHERE IS THE OPPOSITION THAT HAS NOT HURLED BACK THE BRANDING REPROACH OF COLORISM, AGAINST THE MORE ADVANCED OPPOSITION PARTIES, AS WELL AS AGAINST ITS REACTIONARY ADVERSARIES?

TWO THINGS RESULT FROM THIS FACT:

I. COLORISM IS ALREADY ACKNOWLEDGED BY ALL THE WORLD'S POWERS TO BE ITSELF A POWER.

II. IT IS HIGH TIME THAT COLORISTS SHOULD OPENLY, IN THE FACE OF THE WHOLE WORLD, PUBLISH THEIR VIEWS, THEIR AIMS, THEIR TENDENCIES, AND MEET THIS NURSERY TALE OF THE SPECTRUM OF COLOR WITH A MANIFESTO OF THE COLORIST PARTY ITSELF.

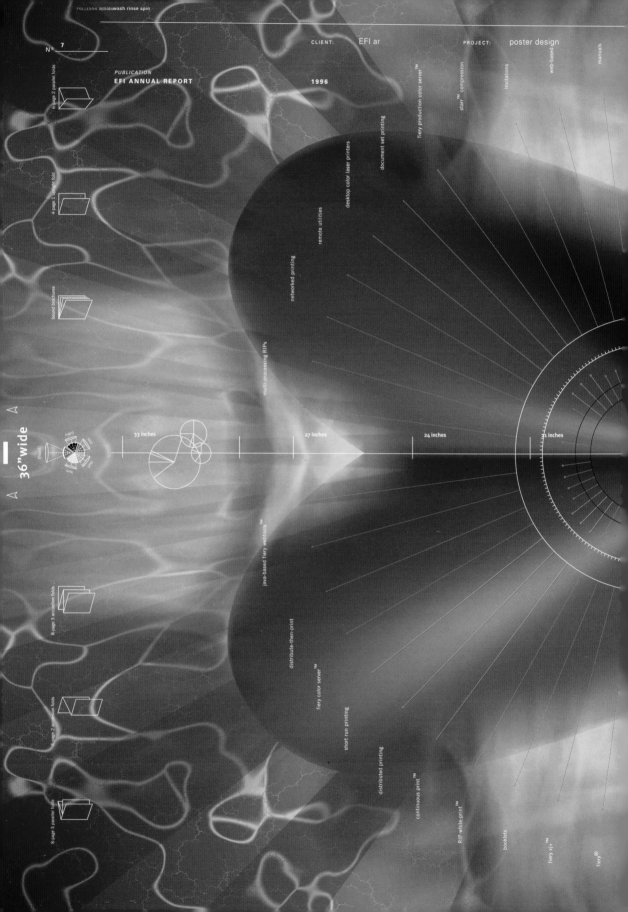

proposal N° 1

brochures

print spooling

presentations

internet printing

RIP-while-print™

fiery x|-w™ wide format printing

finished and imposed documents

high-performance, low cost architecture

scalable from desktop to press

17" (tabloid)

14" (us legal)

11" (us letter)

15 inches

12 inches

9 inches

6 inches

fiery prints™

wide format

on-demand

fiery driven®

fiery x|e™ controller

upgradeable hardware

digital color printing

high-speed digital color copiers

BOURGEOIS AND REVOLUTIONARY COLORISTS
THE HISTORY OF ALL HITHERTO EXISTING SOCIETY IS THE HISTORY OF MONOCHROMATIC VS. MULTI-HUED STRUGGLE. OPPRESSOR AND OPPRESSED STOOD IN CONSTANT OPPOSITION TO ONE ANOTHER, CARRIED ON AN UNINTERRUPTED FIGHT THAT EACH TIME ENDED EITHER IN A REVOLUTIONARY RECONSTITUTION OF SOCIETY AT LARGE, OR IN THE COMMON RUIN OF THE CONTENDING CLASSES.

IN OUR EPOCH, TINTED BY MODERN BOURGEOIS MONOCHROMATIC SOCIETY AND ITS HISTORIC ANTAGONISM AGAINST THOSE SATURATED WITH ENLIGHTENMENT, THE LINES ARE CLEARLY DRAWN. HAVING COMMANDEERED THE MEANS OF OUTPUT PRODUCTION SINCE FEUDAL TIMES, THE BOURGEOIS HAS DRAWN THE TRADITIONAL AGRARIAN COLORIST TO CENTERS OF INDUSTRY, CONVERTING THEM INTO THE INFORMATION WORKING CLASS, AND EXPLOITING THEM AS ITS PAID WAGE LABORERS. IN FORGING THIS LABORING CLASS, THE BOURGEOIS HAVE SOWN THE SEEDS OF ITS OWN DESTRUCTION. IT HAS CALLED INTO EXISTENCE THE PROLETARIANS WHO WIELD THE MEANS OF OUTPUT PRODUCTION — AND WHO NOW COMPRISE THE REVOLUTIONARY COLORISTS!

AS THIS CLASS STRUGGLE ENTERS ITS DECISIVE HOUR, THE PROLETARIANS MUST BECOME MASTERS OF THE PRODUCTIVE COLOR OUTPUT FORCES OF SOCIETY.

PROLETARIANS AND COLORISTS
COLORISTS HAVE NO INTERESTS SEPARATE AND APART FROM THOSE OF THE PROLETARIAT AS A WHOLE. THEY DO NOT SET UP ANY SECTARIAN PRINCIPLES OF THEIR OWN, NO PRISM THROUGH WHICH TO PROJECT THE PROLETARIAN MOVEMENT. COLORISTS ARE THE MOST ADVANCED AND RESOLUTE SECTION OF THE WORKING-CLASS PARTIES OF EVERY COUNTRY. THEIR IMMEDIATE AIM IS FORMATION OF THE PROLETARIAT INTO A CLASS, OVERTHROW OF THE BOURGEOIS MONOCHROMISM, AND A NEW VISIONARY, VIVID WORLD. IN PLACE OF THE OLD DRAB BOURGEOIS SOCIETY, WITH ITS OPPRESSION AND ANTAGONISM, WE SHALL HAVE AN ASSOCIATION IN WHICH THE FREE DEVELOPMENT OF EACH IS THE CONDITION FOR THE FREE COLOR DEVELOPMENT OF ALL.

HENCEFORTH, THE REVOLUTIONARY COLORIST PARTY FIGHTS FOR THE ATTAINMENT OF THE IMMEDIATE AIMS, FOR THE ENFORCEMENT OF THE MOMENTARY INTERESTS OF ALL, MAKING COLOR THE RIGHTFUL COMMON PROPERTY OF ALL. WE OPENLY DECLARE THAT OUR ENDS CAN BE ATTAINED ONLY BY THE FORCIBLE OVERTHROW OF ALL EXISTING MONOCHROMATIC LIMITATIONS AND REPRESSIVE CONDITIONS.

COLLABORATION 1

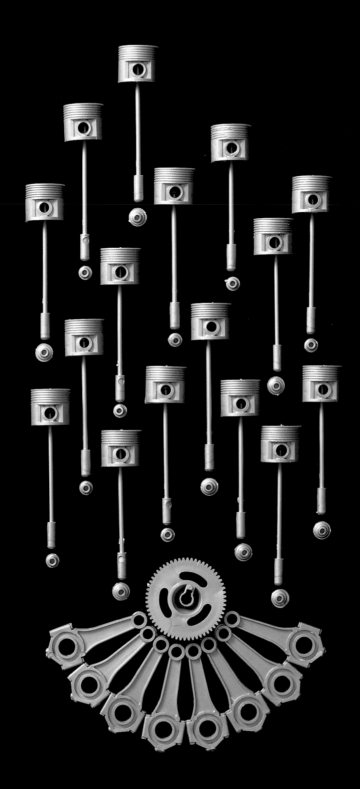

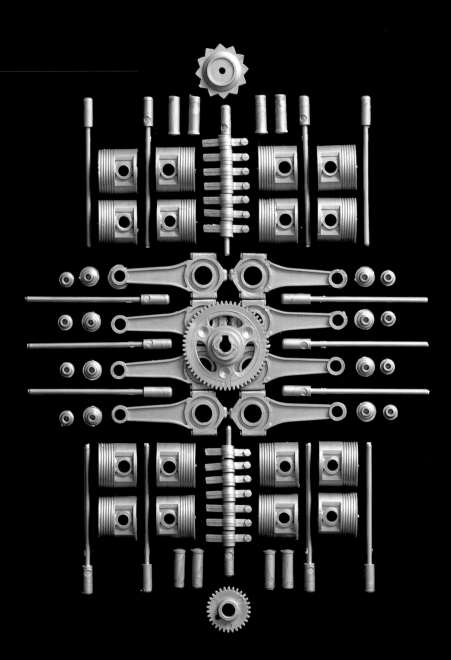

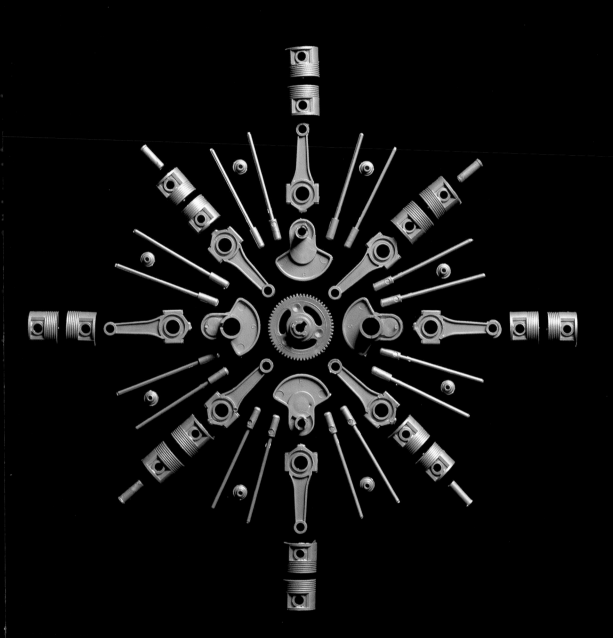

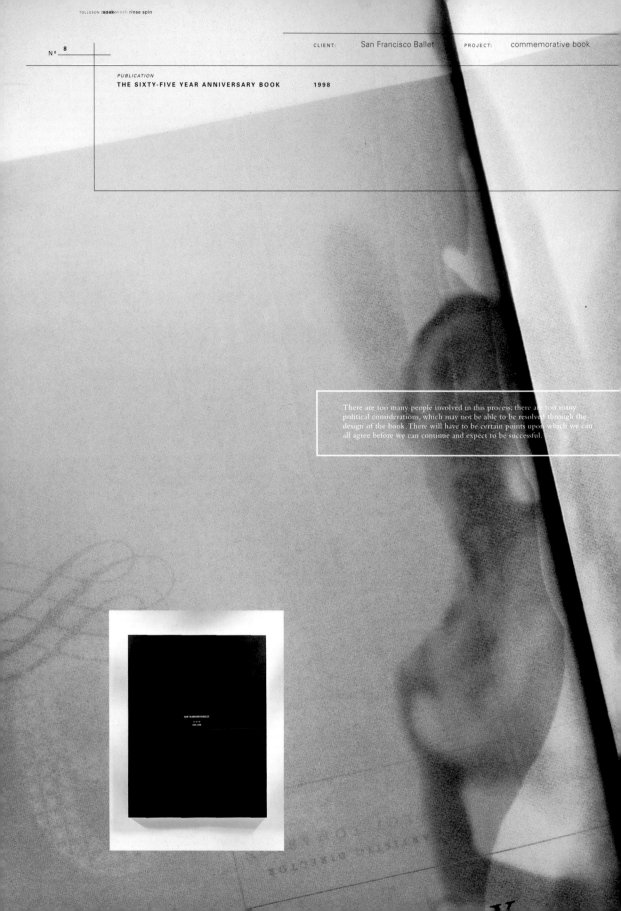

Nº **8**

CLIENT: San Francisco Ballet   PROJECT: commemorative book

PUBLICATION
THE SIXTY-FIVE YEAR ANNIVERSARY BOOK   1998

There are too many people involved in this process; there are too many political considerations, which may not be able to be resolved through the design of the book. There will have to be certain points upon which we can all agree before we can continue and expect to be successful.

To celebrate the 65th anniversary of the troupe, the San Francisco Ballet commissioned a commemorative edition saluting the members of the company past and present and showcased the themes that had been performed throughout the group's history. Intended as a keepsake, the book was presented in acknowledgement of financial patronage at the season's gala opening event.

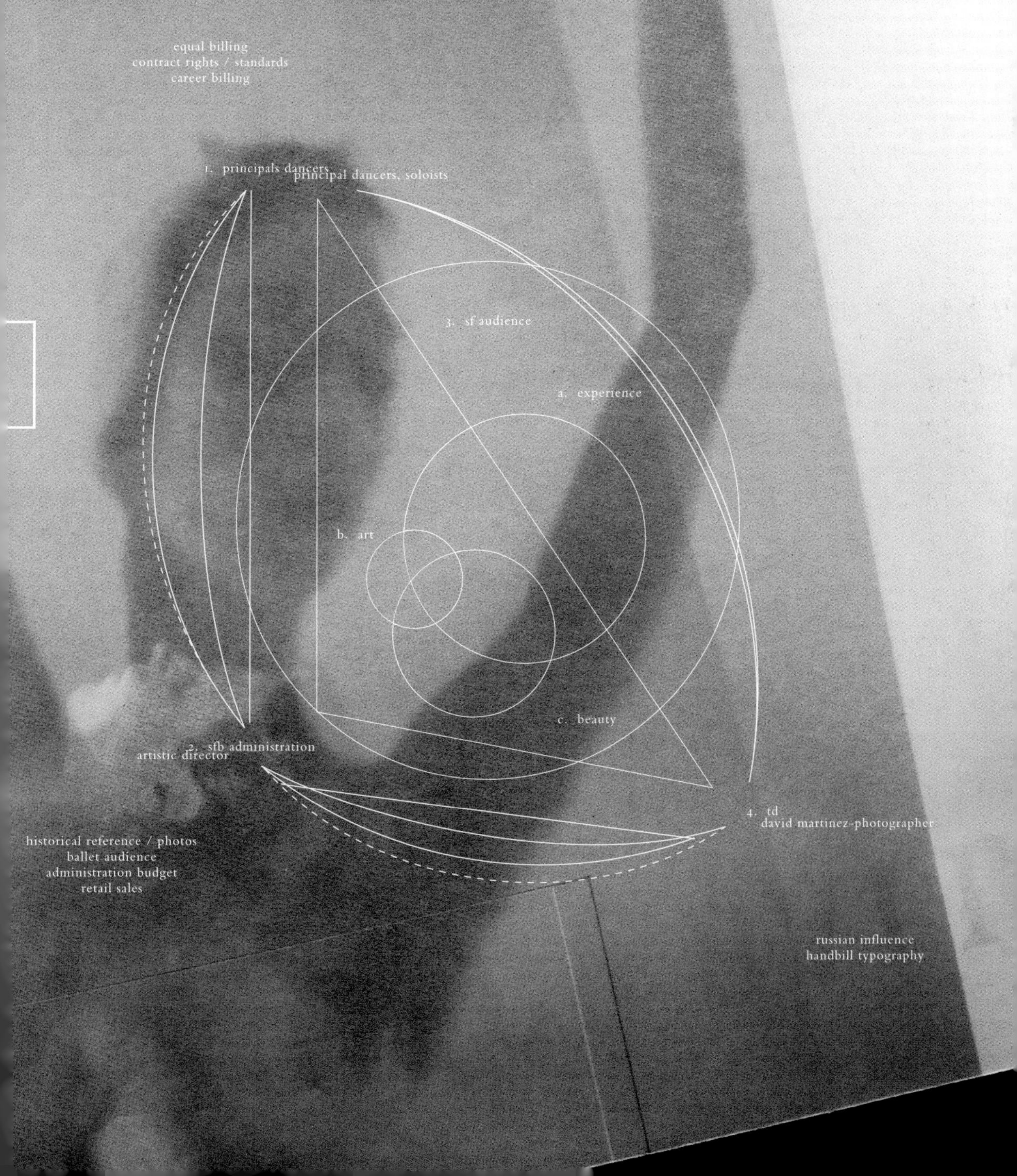

equal billing
contract rights / standards
career billing

1. principals dancers
principal dancers, soloists

3. sf audience

a. experience

b. art

c. beauty

2. sfb administration
artistic director

4. td
david martinez-photographer

historical reference / photos
ballet audience
administration budget
retail sales

russian influence
handbill typography

PUBLICATION
THE SIXTY-FIVE YEAR ANNIVERSARY BOOK   1998

In order to capture the flavor of the dance, the book's typography was structured to surround a stage, set at the center of each spread, around which text, captions and photos revolved as if around the focal point of the performance. A lyrical typographic execution, shaped by historical influences, echoed the graceful movements of the choreography and the lyrical quality of the photography.

ACT 1

PAGES 71~77

CORPS DE BALLET

SAN FRANCISCO BALLET
65

BACKSTAGE 1

STAGE LEFT

STAGE

BALCONY SITE LINE

ORCHESTRA

AUDIENCE

does this look russian?

Helgi's name has to be 50% larger than any other name – it's in her contract!
WHY?

is this supposed to look like an old handbill?

In order to observe the strict hierarchy of the principals, soloists and the corps de ballet, a formality to the placement and pacing of photographs had to be imposed. A dialogue with the Ballet's administrative and publicity staff and the photographer was instrumental in forming a consensus — allowing the images to function as more than snapshots, permitting them to tell their individual stories and relate the artistry of the experience through their poses and costumes.

65th **a.**
San Francisco Ballet
1933 1998
SAN FRANCISCO BALLET
65

NOTES:

_ USE OLD HANDBILL FONTS
_ DON'T LOSE HISTORICAL COMPONENT

NO TEXT   BACKSTAGE 2

STAGE RIGHT

65TH A.
SAN FRANCISCO BALLET
1933~1998
SAN FRANCISCO BALLET
65

all dancers names have to be the same size

i can't believe it, this is awful

how did

st have equal billing   helgi's name must be at least 50 percent as large as sfb

their photos have to be exactly the same size?
evelyn will have a kitten if her name is treated like that

CLIENT: San Francisco Ballet   PROJECT: commemorative book

PUBLICATION
THE SIXTY-FIVE YEAR ANNIVERSARY BOOK   1998

1958

SAN FRANCISCO BALLET
65 BEAUTY AND
THE BEAST

this happen?

we have to airbrush that guy out
soloist can't be one per page, too much like principals
this type is a problem   this font looks too bold

SAN FRANCISCO BALLET
1933~1998

SAN FRANCISCO BALLET
65

65TH A.

she said we could only use the top of this photo
don't make it look so feminine

65TH ANNIVERSARY

SAN FRANCISCO BALLET

HELGI TOMASSON
ARTISTIC DIRECTOR

ARTISTIC DIRECTOR
HELGI TOMASSON

A poster reminiscent of an antique playbill was included at the center of the book. Printed on two sides of a translucent medium, shadowy figures interact as if in rhythm to dances past and present.

she doesn't want us to use that photo
her position isn't perfect

well it's the only photo we have

PUBLICATION
CORPORATE AND PRODUCT LITERATURE   1999

The Genesys story is a story of people, both Genesys people and the people who are their customers. The Genesys product provides accessibility for voice, data and information, and is a faceless technology. To imbue the company that makes human dialog possible with an identity, we developed a brand solution that allows it to show its best face.

CLARENDON REGULAR
abcdefghijklm
nopqrstuvwxyz
0123456789

"hello"

ACCENT COLORS

The success of the Genesys brand endeavor is a result of close collaboration with its customers, and in turn, those customers with customers of their own. To interact with customers, we created a palette of colors, symbols, type and photography that allows the Genesys image to take shape, grow and change along with the needs of its constituency.

PRESSKIT FOLDER

welcome to
genesys

3

4

APPLICATION
THE NORTH FACE BRANDING DOCUMENTS   **1994–1998**

During the course of our 4-year relationship with The North Face, we have worked with product development, marketing, extreme athletes, dealers and retailers and many others to focus and revitalize the brand. Through a series of recurrent cycles, we touched every product developed by The North Face, from conception to testing to marketing. Given the make-up of the decision-making team, the sheer number of players, and the array of items produced by The North Face, we had to be consistent in maintaining the brand message.

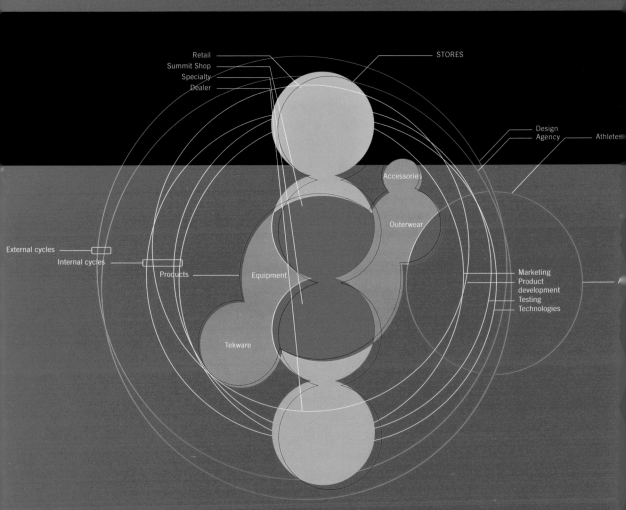

As we evolved The North Face brand, we concentrated on three key attributes that defined the charter of their enterprise: technology & innovation, expedition/heritage and extreme athletes. A company that produces high-performance outerwear, outdoor equipment and functional sportswear and prides itself on its long-standing association with a distinguished team of extreme athletes whose mission it is to continually develop and refine clothing and gear for severe conditions, The North Face has a tradition of integrity and quality that is unsurpassed in the industry.

BRAND STATEMENT:

The North Face is the premier global brand leader in high performance outerwear, outdoor equipment, skiwear and functional sportswear. Independent research shows that The North Face is the most highly rated outdoor brand among consumers and retailers. Consistently ranked as the leader in measures of quality, technical innovation, reputation and brand strength, these high marks are testament to the continued commitment in providing the highest caliber of products and service to the industry.

❶

TECHNOLOGY & INNOVATION

EXTREME ATHLETES ❷

❸ **EXPEDITIONS/ HERITAGE**

❶

TECHNOLOGY & INNOVATION:

The North Face challenges themselves to develop innovative products that establish industry standards across all product categories. With this commitment to technology, they continuously introduce new constructions, designs and fabrics, knowing that no matter how good a product is, it can always be made better. Superior technical fabrics, incredibly durable constructions and function-first designs combine to make their equipment the first choice on many of the world's most challenging expeditions. The North Face puts each fabric and product through rigorous testing standards in the lab, as well as in the field.

❷

EXTREME ATHLETES:

When explorers and serious athletes must trust their lives to their gear, they trust The North Face. The Athletes on The North Face Climbing, Ski, Snowboarding and Endurance Adventure teams share the commitment to technological innovation. Combining their passion for exploration with intimate knowledge of their gear, they are able to help The North Face improve existing designs and develop new ones. Athlete participation is a vital and integral part of both the product engineering and product testing process at The North Face, ensuring that their products perform as well in the mountain as they do in the laboratory.

❸

EXPEDITION HERITAGE:

For 33 years, The North Face has designed and developed equipment that enables individuals to explore the farthest reaches of the earth, as well as close to home, and to experience the exhilaration of challenge and discovery. Their passion for exploration and devotion to technological innovation are the heart of their values and the drivers of their business. The North Face's technological innovations have served countless expeditions, providing critical support to explorers and athletes in pursuit of their goals – from the 1989 American Women's Annapurna expedition, to Helen Thayer's 1988 solo journey to the North Pole, to Greg Child's 1990 ascent of K2. Each expedition has provided The North Face with indispensable ideas and feedback regarding the needs of explorers and the performance of their products.

PUBLICATION
THE NORTH FACE PACKAGING   1994–1998

At The North Face, as with any retail merchandiser, the product cycle is a seasonal one. Through our long association, we became intimately tuned in to the bi-annual timetable dictated by the shift in outdoor activities. We produced a catalog of products, product packaging and in-store concept centers that supported the efforts of retailers, dealers and customers alike. Both the channel and the consumer were our audience as we deployed The North Face's technology story from product development to point of sale.

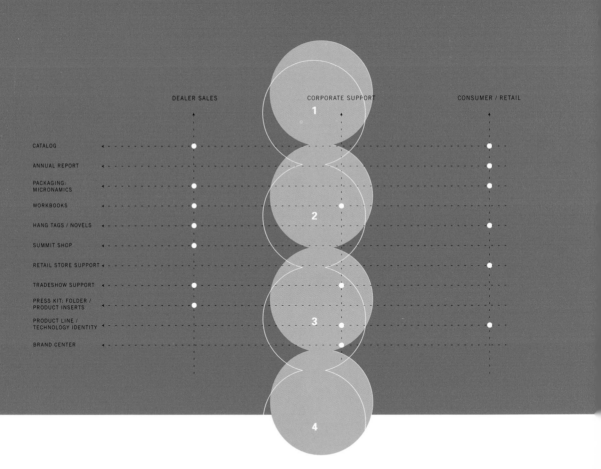

DEALER SALES   CORPORATE SUPPORT   CONSUMER / RETAIL

1

CATALOG

ANNUAL REPORT

PACKAGING:
MICRONAMICS

WORKBOOKS

HANG TAGS / NOVELS   2

SUMMIT SHOP

RETAIL STORE SUPPORT

TRADESHOW SUPPORT

PRESS KIT: FOLDER /
PRODUCT INSERTS

PRODUCT LINE /
TECHNOLOGY IDENTITY   3

BRAND CENTER

4

Specialty packaging was a continual requirement at The North Face. Products constructed of fabric that could not be punctured yet needed to be identified, items so large (i.e.: tents and sleeping bags) they defied traditional means of display, added a new dimension to the creative challenge of merchandising. Finely balanced cards, that allowed each item to be inspected at close range while hanging from its peg, were developed as the packaging for a broad line of accessory items.

PUBLICATION
THE NORTH FACE WORKBOOKS   1994–1998

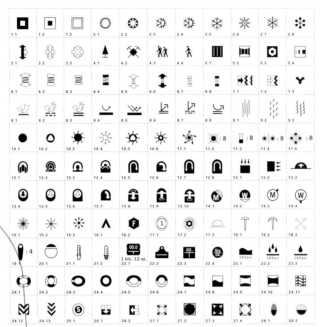

1   Fabric Layers
2   Seasons
3   Micro Fit Series
4   Pack Usage
5   Zipper Construction
6   Fill Power
7   Zip-in Construction
8   Waterproof / Windproof
9   Fabric Breathability
10 Polarguard
11 Number of Poles
12 Pack Lid Conversion
13 Pack Access
14 Men / Women
15 Goose Fill Rating
16 Tent Footprint
17 Tent Gear loft #
18 Climbing Gear Rating
19 Tent Capacity
20 Tent Vestibule
21 Temperature Rating
22 Weight
23 Pressure Rating
24 Fabric Construction
25 Small Sizes
26 Pack Access
27 Capacity
28 Color

Climb Very Light Jacket

At a mere 18 ounces, our no-frills Climb Very Light Jacket with Gore-Tex® 3-ply fabric is
engineered to achieve maximum function per ounce. It is the ultimate in weight-saving
protection for serious outdoor activities in heavy rain and wind. The Climb Very Light
features our ergonomic swivel hood that adjusts with one hand, a high collar that pro-
tects the neck and chin, articulated elbows, and generous seamless shoulder construction for unrestricted movement. Also available as an Anorak.

Gore-Tex 3-ply Fabric with Lightweight Nylon Ripstop

00.0 : 1 lb 2 oz   (M) XS S M L XL XXL   (W) S M L XL

VaporWick

Hydroseal

UltraWick

Double XX

Abrasion / Water

To facilitate consumer identification of product features, we standardized a language
of product icons and fabric illustrations. Describing everything from insulation value to
gusset style, these little identifiers functioned as a sort of shorthand - in the catalog,
on product hangtags and virtually all marketing literature - that aided in garment and
equipment selection.

DIR. N° **2.⁰ / 2.¹**

spring 98
technical outerwear

spring 98
ascentials

Small volumes describing product features and benefits as well as care instructions were devised for each line of clothing and outdoor gear.

women's tekware

women's tekware

big wall gear

big wall gear

As a preview of the coming line, product workbooks are issued to dealers and merchants. From these minimal descriptions and line illustrations of new product offerings, the buyer selects the inventory he will stock. Elaborate catalogs portraying a selection of items in full-color are also supplied as the garments ship to the stores. Items not stocked can be offered to a customer on a special order basis. This system allows The North Face to respond quickly to the changing environment and to limit the consumption of more costly print materials.

N° **10**

CLIENT: The North Face   PROJECT: catalog

PUBLICATION
THE NORTH FACE CATALOG   1998

DIR. N°   **4**.0

APPLICATION
SUMMIT SHOP SIGNAGE PROGRAM   **1994–1998**

88 MT. EVEREST

Technically advanced outerwear for the place that needs it most: the head. Designed for serious cold and wet weather activities requiring breathability, warmth and overall protection from inclement weather.

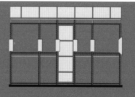

TENT DISPLAY   FOUR-WAY HANG DISPLAY   WALL DISPLAY   TWO-WAY HANG DISPL

The design of Summit Shops (store within store concept centers) extend the reach of The North Face brand into the retail environment. These installations, along with dedicated North Face retail stores, have been specially outfitted with fixtures, graphics and educational installations in support of the Expedition Heritage campaign. Floor covering resembling a topographic surface (showing first ascents and descents of the world's major peaks), larger-than-life athlete pylons and even an early prototype of a backpack that climbed Mt. Everest (and survived to tell its tale) complete the environment as you experience a North Face installation.

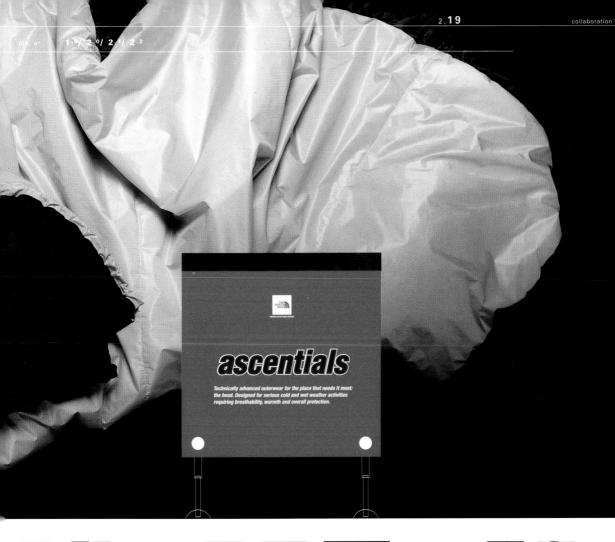

ascentials

Technically advanced outerwear for the place that needs it most: the head. Designed for serious cold and wet weather activities requiring breathability, warmth and overall protection.

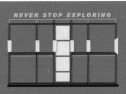

THREE-SIDED MERCHANDISING UNIT   CUBE UNIT   WALL DISPLAY

Designers designing for designers. It seems a natural enough fit. In reality it can be quite a challenging situation. To depict the products developed by IDEO without adding anything to the presentation that could distract or detract from the pure experience of those forms proved an exercise in respectful restraint.

IDEO imbued us with a sense of their own design philosophy as they relinquished images of the prototypes to be included in the monograph. The booklet was designed as if it were itself an archetype for an original product. The visuals of the objects we were supplied were to be the only design elements. Any other ingredients were grudgingly admitted into the composition. Typography had to be simple, quiet and appropriate, absolutely unobtrusive and non-competitive with the poetry of lines in a computer monitor, or the fluid outline of a table leg.

To measure the expression of all the elements essential to the solution so precisely was to create a symphony of pieces in which no single voice could be heard above another. Shaping the pages became a study in minimalism during which the sizing and cropping of each photo took on the precision of a surgeon's stroke.

A7PS

ＡLP

CIRCA	WEIGHT	PRODUCT	MATERIALS	WEIGHT				CIRCA
1997	24 LB 14 OZ	FIG TABLE **STEELCASE** ALUMINUM		4 LB 1 OZ	7	**NEC**	12	1997
	DIMENSIONS		STEEL	DIMENSIONS				
	24 × 17 × 32		CARBON	24 × 17 × 5				
	24 × 14 × 18							

PUBLICATION
PORTFOLIO 98

CLIENT: IDEO   PROJECT: product yearbook

PRODUCT STAGE

PRODUCT   1   2   3   3

CRITICAL INFORMATION : COMPANY ID, PRODUCT ID, SPECS, DESCRIPTION

PACING : 1 1 1 2 1 2 3 4 5 8 9 0 5 6 7

CRITERIA :
1. MUST REVEAL DESIGN PHILOSOPHY
2. MUST REFER TO DESIGN PROCESS
3. FRAME AND STAGE PRODUCT
4. CONSIDER PRINTED PIECE AS PRODUCT
5. DISTILL COMPLEXITY TO MINIMUM

ALPS 1   ALPS

PRODUCT	MATERIALS		CIRCA		WEIGHT		MATERIALS
X.L 17	PLASTIC ZINC		1997	**SAMSUNG** PRODUCT DX.L 17	4 LB 1 OZ DIMENSIONS 24 × 17 × 5		TITANIUM FE

samsung

CLIENT: IDEO   PROJECT: product yearbook

CLIENT: Cyan, Broderbund Software   PROJECT: id / packaging

PUBLICATION
PACKAGING AND PROMOTIONS   1997

The roots of the age of Myst can be traced back through time to a world called D'ni (pronounced Dunny). For reasons not yet revealed, the D'ni world was destroyed and the inhabitants escaped to other worlds they had written, as well as to Earth. Riven, the sequel to Myst, takes place in the Fifth Age written by Gehn. Visually, the world of Riven is infused with Victorian sensibilities, Persian ornamentation, and lore of the Middle Ages; overlaying this historic allusion is the influence of a futuristic technology.

Designing the identity for Riven evolved into a collaborative affiliation between the creator/producer (Cyan), distributor (Broderbund) and designer. Work advanced simultaneously on the interactive interface, the logotype and the product packaging. At the same time, the marketing contingent was at work creating "hype" around the release through announcements to the press, that, in turn, influenced the product under development.

This parallel development cycle provided a rich exchange of ideas and concepts but, at the same time, it was an effort to align all of the various instincts and interests seamlessly.

From our previous projects with Cyan, and Robin and Rand Miller in particular, we were familiar with their critical eye and sensitivity surrounding the creative process. Juxtaposed against their continual struggle to improve the product, was Broderbund's concern that this product sell. As we spent time refining and exploring many elements of the design and experience, Broderbund was market testing the variations that evolved. Positioned in the middle of this dynamic, we often acted as the "glue" or the go-between, helping to interpret input and keep the process moving forward.

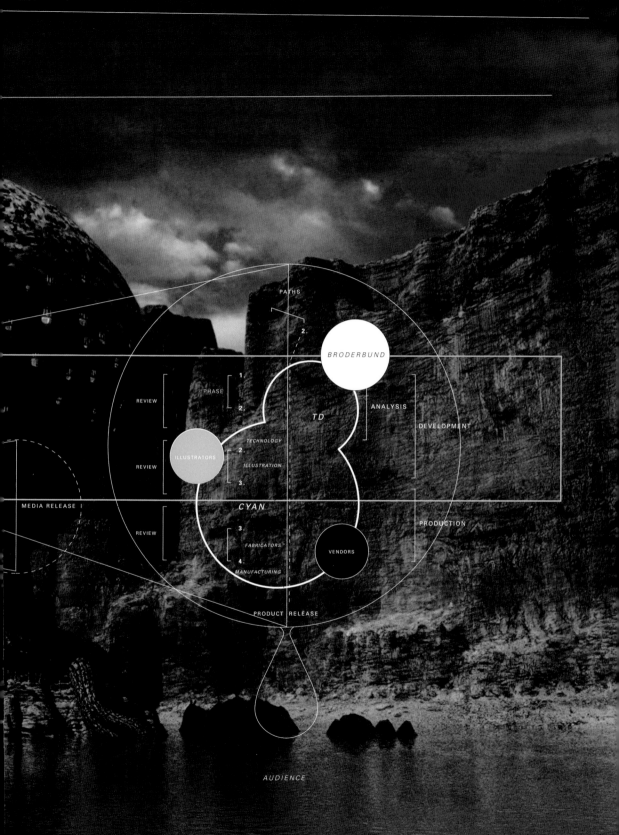

PATHS

2.

BRODERBUND

1.

PHASE

2.   *TD*   ANALYSIS

REVIEW   DEVELOPMENT

                    TECHNOLOGY

2.

REVIEW   ILLUSTRATORS   *ILLUSTRATION*

3.

                    CYAN

MEDIA RELEASE   PRODUCTION

3.

REVIEW   *FABRICATORS*   VENDORS

4.

                    MANUFACTURING

PRODUCT RELEASE

AUDIENCE

The number 5 figures largely in the D'ni culture; i.e. five-sided rooms, numbering system in base five — hence the visual emphasis on the central character in the Riven title. Graphical elements and patterns were also borrowed from antique Persian and Celtic motifs.

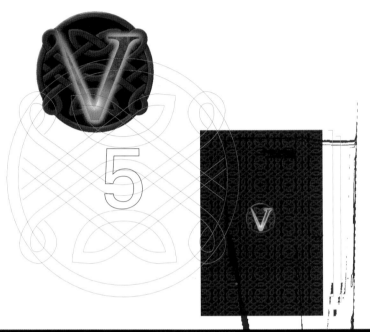

1.
2.

ABOVE: **MONOGRAM MARK**
BELOW: **LOGOTYPE WITH BACKING**

DIR. N°   **1**.0

COLOR STUDIES
Once the titling was set, a multitude of studies drew on colors from within the work of Riven. It was imperative that subtle shifts in color be achievable not only in RGB for the screen applications but also in CMYK for print media.

CLUES   **P.O.P.**

TRAVEL   **ADS**

PUZZLES   **PACKAGING**

RECORDS   **MERCHANDISING**

TRAVEL   **CD**

1.0

R I V E N
SEQUEL TO MYST

R I V E N
SEQUEL TO MYST

R I V E N
SEQUEL TO MYST

R I V E N
SEQUEL TO MYST

2.0

SPECTRUM   1.25   2.25

R I V E N
SEQUEL TO MYST

R I V E N
SEQUEL TO MYST   3.25   4.25

R I V E N
SEQUEL TO MYST   5.25   6.25

R I V E N
SEQUEL TO MYST   7.25   8.25

3.0

R I V E N
SEQUEL TO MYST

R I V E N
SEQUEL TO MYST

R I V E N
SEQUEL TO MYST

R I V E N
SEQUEL TO MYST

4.0

R I V E N
SEQUEL TO MYST

R I V E N
SEQUEL TO MYST

R I V E N
SEQUEL TO MYST

R I V E N
SEQUEL TO MYST

5.0

R I V E N
SEQUEL TO MYST

R I V E N
SEQUEL TO MYST

R I V E N
SEQUEL TO MYST

R I V E N
SEQUEL TO MYST

6.0

R I V E N
SEQUEL TO MYST

R I V E N
SEQUEL TO MYST

R I V E N
SEQUEL TO MYST

R I V E N
SEQUEL TO MYST

N° **12**

CLIENT: Cyan, Broderbund Software   PROJECT: id / packaging

PUBLICATION
PACKAGING AND PROMOTIONS   1997

rev.02   rev.11

rev.12   rev.27

CLUE No. 1   CLUE No. 2

ENCRYPT

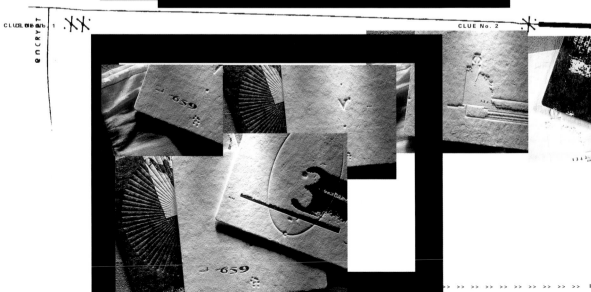

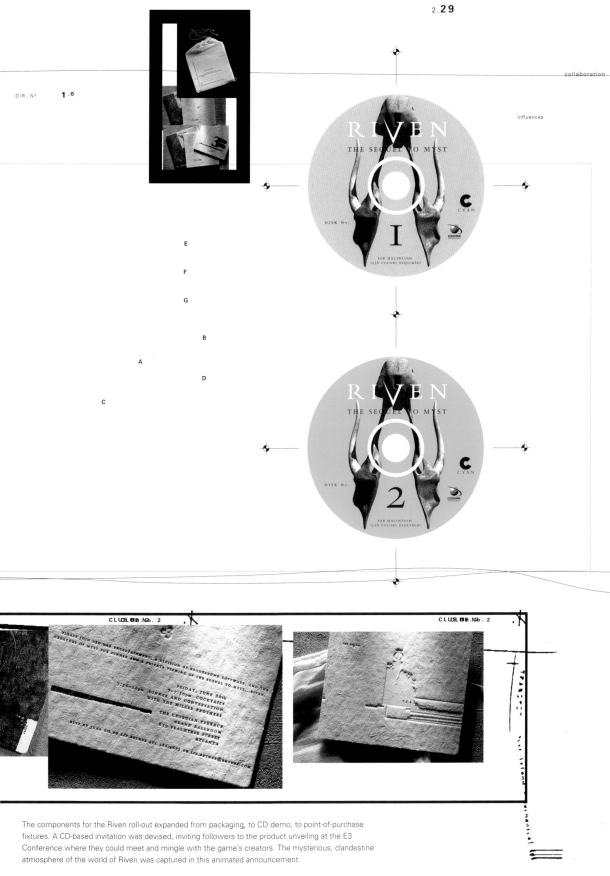

DIR. Nº   **1**.⁰

The components for the Riven roll-out expanded from packaging, to CD demo, to point-of-purchase fixtures. A CD-based invitation was devised, inviting followers to the product unveiling at the E3 Conference where they could meet and mingle with the game's creators. The mysterious, clandestine atmosphere of the world of Riven was captured in this animated announcement.

CLIENT: Cyan, Broderbund Software   PROJECT: id / packaging

PUBLICATION
PACKAGING AND PROMOTIONS

1997

FRAME .07 SEC

FRAME .08 SEC

FRAME .11 SEC

FRAME .1.22 SEC

FRAME .1.23 SEC

FRAME .1.29 SEC

FRAME .1.46 SEC

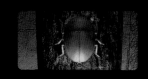

FRAME .1.48 SEC

FRAME .1.49 SEC

FRAME .2.03 SEC

FRAME .2.24 SEC

FRAME .2.35 SEC

FRAME .**28** SEC

FRAME .**40** SEC

FRAME .**50** SEC

FRAME .**1.33** SEC

FRAME .**1.35** SEC

FRAME .**1.38** SEC

FRAME .**1.50** SEC

FRAME .**1.55** SEC

FRAME .**1.59** SEC

FRAME .**2.43** SEC

FRAME .**2.54** SEC

FRAME .**2.55** SEC

CLIENT: Urban Outfitters   PROJECT: print / web site

APPLICATION
1998 ANNUAL REPORT CONCEPTS   1998–1999

As we approached the concept development for the 1998 Urban Outfitters annual report, our aims were to in some way play off the pseudo-pharma-ceutical environments of that year's retail stores, and to imbue the visual portion of the document with a decidedly urban nature.

DIR. 1   **DIR. 2**

DIR. 3   **DIR. 4**   **DIR. 5**

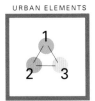

CONCEPT #1 — ALCHEMY:
SCIENTIFIC DISCOVERIES MADE USING COMMON HOUSEHOLD PRODUCTS
TYPICAL EVERYDAY ITEMS ARE COMBINED TO FORM UNIQUE COMPOUNDS WITH DISTINCTLY PECULIAR PROPERTIES. FOR INSTANCE: WHEN MIXED, DANDELION BUDS, DRYER LINT AND BOTTLED WATER WERE FOUND TO CREATE AN ENERGY DRINK POWERFUL ENOUGH TO MAKE OLYMPIC ATHLETES FROM COUCH POTATOES. SIMILARLY, ASBESTOS BRAKE DUST FROM RAPID TRANSIT TRAINS HAS BEEN FOUND TO ENHANCE PHEROMONE PRODUCTION TO A SUCH DEGREE THAT COMMUTERS CAN BE SEEN LEAVING THE COMPARTMENTS TWO-BY-TWO (A LA NOAH'S ARK).

CONCEPT #3 — THE SCIENCE OF FASHION:
TESTS FOR THE CLOTHING OF TODAY
SCIENTIFIC EXPERIMENTS ARE CONDUCTED TO DEMONSTRATE THE DURABILITY OF ANY NUMBER OF "POPULAR" GARMENTS. THE MOHAIR "FUZZY" SWEATER HAS BEEN PUT THROUGH ITS PACES AND HAS BEEN FOUND TO WITHSTAND 200 MAKE-OUT SESSIONS. LIKEWISE, A PAIR OF DENIM JEANS HAS BEEN RATED TO WITHSTAND SKATEBOARD ROAD-RASH FAR BETTER THAN THE COMPETITOR'S CHINOS. A NEW FABRIC HAS BEEN PROVEN TO BE DRINK-RESISTANT AND WILL NOT REEK AFTER A WEEK'S EXPOSURE TO SECOND-HAND CIGARETTE SMOKE.

CONCEPT #5 — URBAN MYTHS AND LEGENDS: AN URBAN LEGEND APPEARS MYSTERIOUSLY AND SPREADS SPONTANEOUSLY; THEY ARE RARELY TRUE, BUT FOR GOOD STORYTELLING.

THESE STORIES ABOUND. WE ALL HAVE HEARD THE ONE ABOUT THE ALLIGATOR IN THE SEWER SYSTEM OR LITTLE MIKEY WHO CONSUMED A LETHAL DOSE OF POP ROCKS AND COKE OR THOSE EELSKIN BILLFOLDS WHICH CONFOUNDED BANKERS BY SCRAMBLING MAGNETIC CODES ON ATM AND CREDIT CARDS. THE URBAN ENVIRONMENT IS FERTILE GROUND FOR OUTRAGEOUSLY PLAUSIBLE TALES.

CONCEPT #4 — SOCIAL SCIENCE 101:
A CORE SAMPLE OF THE URBAN ENVIRONMENT

A BORE IS MADE IN THE YEAR 2,900 AND, WHEN THE CORE IS WITHDRAWN, IT IS FOUND TO CONTAIN A PLETHORA OF ARTIFACTS REPRESENTATIVE OF ALL THE DECADES OF CIVILIZATION. THE ITEMS CONTAINED IN THE SLICE ARE INDICATIVE OF THE SCIENTIFIC, CULTURAL, MUSICAL, FASHION, HISTORIC, SOCIOLOGICAL AND DEMOGRAPHIC CLIMATE OF THE TIME.

CONCEPT #2 — PERIODIC CHART OF PERSONALITIES:
HUMAN BEINGS ARE ASSIGNED THE POSITIONS AND PROPERTIES OF VARIOUS ELEMENTS IN THE PERIODIC TABLE

A PARODY OF THE PERIODIC CHART OF ELEMENTS IS GENERATED AND HERE'S THE TWIST— EACH CELL ON THE CHART CONTAINS A HUMAN ILLUSTRATED TO PERSONIFY A PARTICULAR SET OF ELEMENTAL CHARACTERISTICS. WHATEVER THE HYDROGEN MAN TOUCHES SPON- TANEOUSLY BURSTS INTO FLAME; THE URANIUM WOMAN CAUSES FLOWERS TO WILT AS SHE PASSES; THE HELIUM BOY FLOATS AWAY HAVING BROKEN HIS TETHER.

When presented with these possible scenarios for the foundation of the book, Urban Outfitters simply asked that we "make the book look good." In this instance, the concept was deemed to be of secondary importance to the overall impact of the piece. Design was paramount. They liked the work they'd seen in the portfolio and wanted us to take the project and run with it. We took inspiration from more than one of the concepts relating to the scientific and implemented a miniature volume that captured a distinctly urban character.

A slightly uncommon relationship ensued. Our initial contact with Urban Outfitters was through a call to send our portfolio. Once they awarded us the project, our subsequent conversations were via telephone, and all presentations were couriered; to this day, we have not met with the client face-to-face. Even so, it still feels as though we've come to know our contacts well and have established an association that allows for seamless communication across the miles.

CLIENT: Urban Outfitters   PROJECT: annual report

PUBLICATION
**1998 URBAN OUTFITTERS
ANNUAL REPORT**

STMPS.1

4-5

10-11

46-47

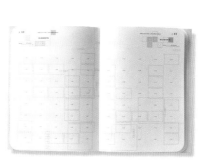

48-49

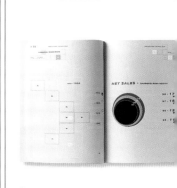

c

DIR. Nº   6.0

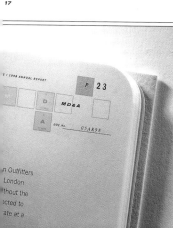

N° 13

CLIENT: Urban Outfitters   PROJECT: annual report

PUBLICATION
1999 URBAN OUTFITTERS ANNUAL REPORT   1999

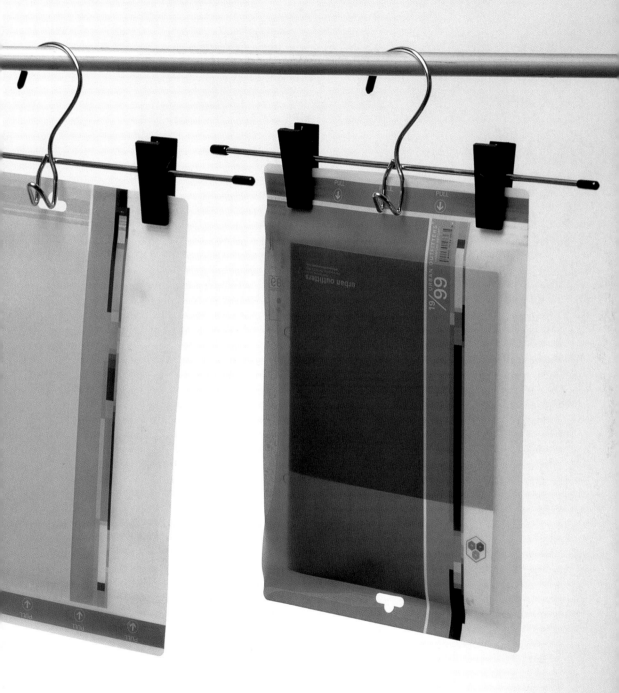

PUBLICATION
1999 URBAN OUTFITTERS ANNUAL REPORT   1999

The next year, once again given the caveat to design at will, we decided to define the annual report as though it were itself a product. Monochromatic vertical bars overprint catalog photography as though they'd been processed by a bar-scanner, reminiscent of the graphic style of the electronic demo. Printed on plastic and sealed inside a plastic wrapper, the package appeared as though it might have been selected from the shelves of a department store.

1309

URBAN WHOLESALE

| Customers | 1309 |
| Brands | 3 |
| 1. free people |
| 2. bulldog |
| 3. co-operative mfg. co |

Urban Outfitters Wholesale Division designs and sells women's apparel under three brand labels to 1,309 stores. Bulldog, Free People, and Co-op brands are sold to better retail stores throughout the United States, Canada and Japan.

3×

CLIENT: Urban Outfitters   PROJECT: website design

PUBLICATION
URBAN OUTFITTERS WEBSITE   1998

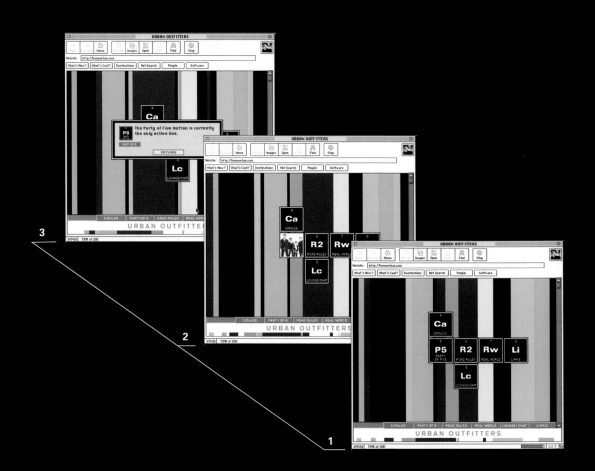

3

2

1

1 - HOME ANIMATION
2 - TOC
3 - UNDER CONSTRUCTION
4 - PARTY OF FIVE INTRO PAGE
5 - NEVE CAMPBELL PAGE
6 - SHOPPING PAGE
7 - SHOPPING CART / ORDER

During the down time between annual reports, we collaborated on an interactive demo of the
Urban Outfitters e-commerce site. The site features a series of cycling stripes, inspired by the
repeat pattern in product bar codes. These dancing bars serve as a backdrop for a periodic chart
of "The Party of 5," whose stars regularly model a selection of current Urban Outfitters styles.

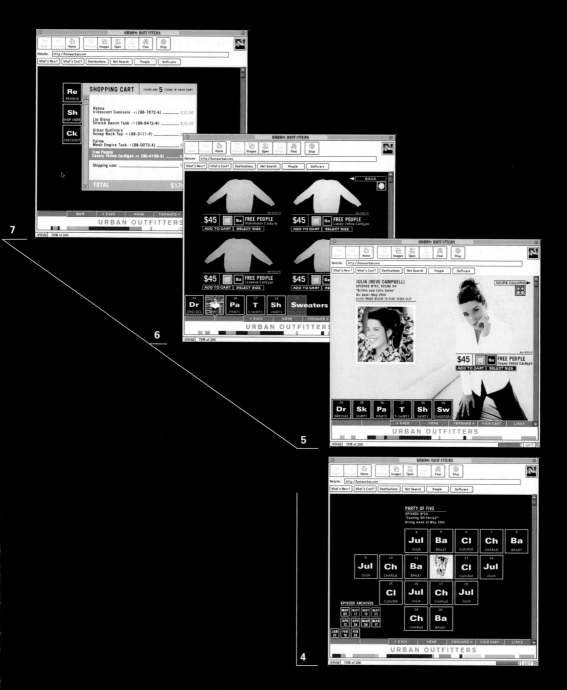

7

6

5

4

CLIENT: Sharpe Associates PROJECT: Photography promo

PUBLICATION
COMPILATION : NEW WORK VOLS. 1 - 3 1997

JS:
JOHN SHARPE AND ASSOCIATES

EW:
EVERARD WILLIAMS, JR.

NB:
NEIL BROWN

JS:
JAMEY STILLINGS

HK:
HUGH KRETCHSMER

TD:
TOLLESON DESIGN

JS

J S

n-b

OPTION
THEME
OPTION 2
SPACE

TD

COMPILATION: NEW WORK

NO TIME
N — E
W — S
TIME

To achieve a collaborative feeling among the five disparate portfolios represented by Sharpe + Associates, we built a photography promotional brochure as one would assemble a gallery showing. Initially we considered a concept for the promotion in which each photographer was assigned to interpret a common theme, *TOUCH*. However, trying to coordinate availabilities proved too difficult an assignment, so we conceived the gallery approach as a neutral environment to show off the works in their best light.

Envisioned as a white backdrop against which the five unique styles could share the spotlight, the open context of the gallery framed the works and afforded each its own space. A make-ready sheet proved a solution to package the mailing. Images collaged randomly over a translucent sheet were then folded down to form a carrier for the catalog. Opening the package created a sensation similar to unveiling a work of art in a show. The compilation of styles on the exterior wrap hinted at the varied collection of images featured inside.

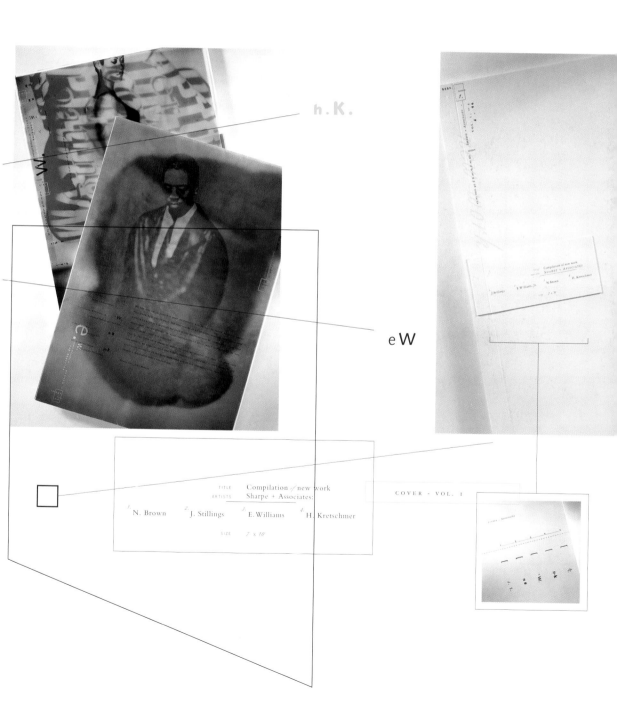

h.K.

eW

TITLE   Compilation *of* new work
ARTISTS   Sharpe + Associates:

N. Brown   J. Stillings   E.Williams   H. Kretschmer

SIZE   *7 x 10*

COVER - VOL. 1

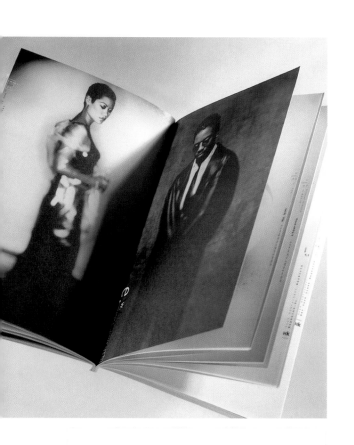

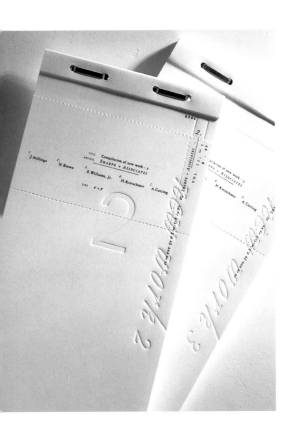

BOOK 2 · PH. 2 · IMAGE 2.2 of 4

PUBLICATION
HOLIDAY PAPER

DIR. Nº **1.0 / 8.0**

PROJECT: wrapping paper

CLIENT: Watermark Press

1997, 1998

Nº **15**

Each year the studio has the opportunity to design a series of gift wrapping papers that are distributed as a holiday promotion by Watermark Press. Since the papers are intended to show off the printer's capabilities, there are few restrictions or guidelines.

Once we establish a basis in content, color and design, the artwork is passed along from hand to hand until all the sheets have been touched by each contributor. The patterns are enriched in visual and intellectual content — and wit — as they're turned over from one designer to the next in our studio.

x-8

next new thing

x-8 can bring children hours of unconditional happiness

BATTERY OPERATED BEST FRIEND

x-8
next new thing

0 1 2 3 4 5 6 7 8 9

CLIENT: GATX Capital   PROJECT: cd / annual reports

APPLICATION
GATX CAPITAL INTERACTIVE CAPABILITIES CD   1995, 1996

To develop an interactive CD for GATX Capital to include in their 1995 annual report, we needed to get inside the company and learn the inner-workings of its many business groups. GATX is composed of a number of sales arms, each selling into a unique market segment. Previously these groups sold to their individual customers in different manners using separate sales tools. Unifying the entire sales and marketing effort through the single vehicle of the CD was quite an accomplishment.

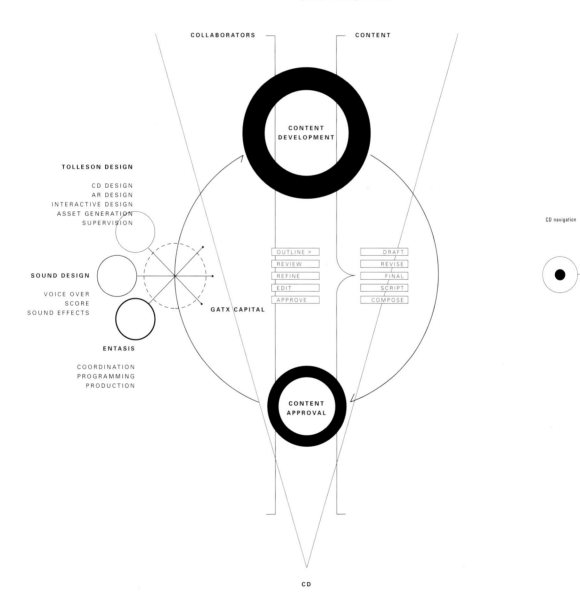

COLLABORATORS   CONTENT

CONTENT
DEVELOPMENT

TOLLESON DESIGN

CD DESIGN
AR DESIGN
INTERACTIVE DESIGN
ASSET GENERATION
SUPERVISION

SOUND DESIGN

VOICE OVER
SCORE
SOUND EFFECTS

GATX CAPITAL

ENTASIS

COORDINATION
PROGRAMMING
PRODUCTION

OUTLINE >   DRAFT
REVIEW   REVISE
REFINE   FINAL
EDIT   SCRIPT
APPROVE   COMPOSE

CONTENT
APPROVAL

CD navigation

CD

The information architecture of the CD had to accommodate a broad range of
needs and styles. The content diagram and navigation system were based on the
GATX corporate structure, groups working within other groups — multiple hubs
through which information could be accessed at random across business lines.

We were involved in a further collaboration with Entasis, an interactive production
company, whose expertise we employed to program the interactive component of
the project. In addition, we subcontracted with copywriters and sound studios to
achieve voice and special effects.

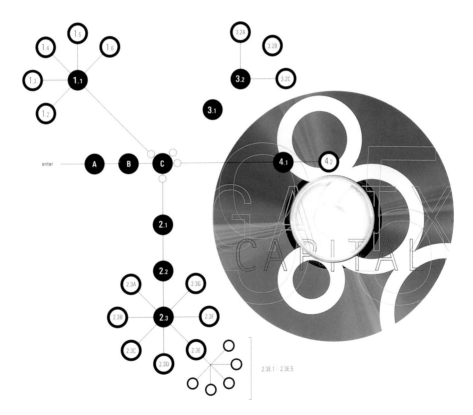

CD Content Structure	A - GATX Capital Home Page	1.1 - Annual Report cover	2.1 - Company Overview	3.1 - Transaction Highlights	4.1 - Offices
	B - President's Letter	1.2 - AR table of contents	2.2 - Introduction	3.2 - Introduction	4.2 - Maps and address
	C - Site contents	1.3 - Charts	2.3 - GATX Capital groups	3.2A - Transaction 1	information
		1.4 - President's letter	2.3A - GATX Air	3.2B - Transaction 2	
		1.5 - Business review	2.3B - GATX Rail	3.2C - Transaction 3	
		1.6 - Financials	2.3C - Corporate Finance		
			2.3D - GATX Golf Capital		
			2.3E - Joint ventures		
			GARM/UK		
			GARM/Canada		
			GATX/CL Air		
			GATX-Airlog		
			AARM		
			2.3F - GATX EnviroLease		
			2.3G - Technology Finance		

CLIENT: GATX Capital PROJECT: cd / annual reports

APPLICATION
GATX CAPITAL INTERACTIVE CAPABILITIES CD 1995, 1996

23 SEC OPENING COMPOSITION   **55 SEC TITLE SEQUENCE**   **60 SEC CONTENT SE**

3:20 SEC JOINT VENTURE   **3:25 SEC SECTION CONTENT**   **4:37 SEC SECTION TRAN**

7:30 SEC SECTION CONTENT   **7:32 SEC SECTION TRANSITION**   **8:00 SEC ANNUAL REPORT MA**

EQUIPMENT

EQUIPMENT INFORMATION

EQUIPMENT ANNUAL REPORT

EQUIPMENT

EQUIPMENT TRANSACTION

EQUIPMENT

EQUIPMENT

1:02 SEC CONTENT SELECTOR **1:06 SECTION CONTENT** **3:06 SECTION TRANSITION**

ENVIRONMENTAL

ENVIRONMENTAL
INFORMATION

ENVIRONMENTAL
ANNUAL REPORT

STRENGTHS
ENVIRONMENTAL

4:40 SEC JOINT VENTURE **6:02 SECTION CONTENT** **6:07 SECTION TRANSITION**

READING RATES

TRANSACT

TRINITY

GC CN
66 060
FF

SEC CASE STUDY SECTION TITLE SEQUENCE **10:20 TRANSACTION CASE STUDY TITLE** **12:30 DIRECTORY**

APPLICATION
GATX CAPITAL INTERACTIVE CAPABILITIES CD   1995, 1996

INTERNAL COLLABORATION

While the 1995 project required an extensive internal collaboration, uniting all the working factions within GATX with a common agenda, the 1996 annual report focused on external associations — GATX's working relationships with its business partners and subsidiaries. Throughout the course of the book, their alliances with corporate associates and affiliates are defined and examined in light of the company's major areas of business.

APPLICATION

GATX CAPITAL INTERACTIVE CAPABILITIES CD   1995, 1996

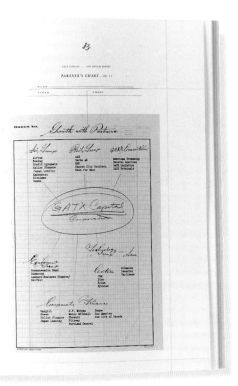

PUBLICATION
COTTONG AND TANIGUCHI PORTFOLIO   **1993 - 1999**

Among the clients with whom we have long-standing relationships are Cottong & Taniguchi, a landscape architectural company. In 1991, we first conceived their identity, a monogram based on a sprouting seedling, and designed their business papers, employing specimen-like typography — all in keeping with the nature of their business. We then followed with a mail promotion that featured project drawings representing a variety of categories, packaged inside small seed packets.

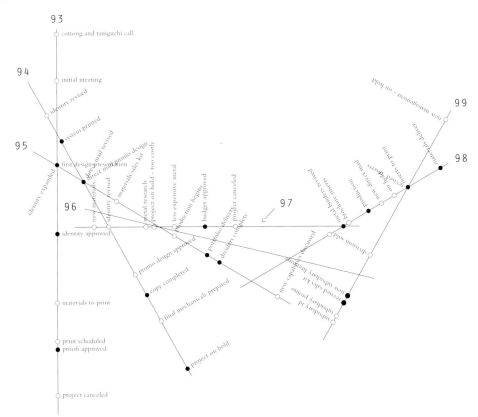

Our relationship has continued into this year — it has not been a linear one, however. Once the initial suite of materials was in place, the pattern of our association with Cottong & Taniguchi took on a start/stop dynamic. This was due to a number of internal, as well as extraneous forces, which affected the cultivation of their business and the direction of its growth.

Early in our alliance, we agreed on a structured program of marketing materials. The goal of this package was to help Cottong & Taniguchi attract projects of larger scope and magnitude. To sell to this customer, we needed a system that was readily customizable. We created a binder format with re-configurable divider pages and project cut sheets.

DIR. Nº   **1**·⁰

» MONOGRAM SYMBOL «   1

» PALETTE «

2

» IDENTITY APPLICATIONS «   3

5435u	5497u	5565u	5625u	5773u	5777u	5855u	5835
436u	437u	438u	443u	444u	5565u	5425u	367u
103u	110u	173u	457u	458u	465u	471u	472u	4725u	480u
611u	612u	617u	618u	721u	716u	727u
401u	402u	403u	407u	408u	409u	413u	414u	415u	421u	422u	423u

442u	443u	617u	5855u	5435u	138u	129u		438u	5507u
5835u	5777u	5565u	5773u	5497u	5425u	472u
436u	437u				173u	457u
					458u	465u

                    A   B   C · E
P » BUSINESS SYSTEM « 94   P » MAIL PROMOTION 1 « 92   P » SALES MATERIALS « 99

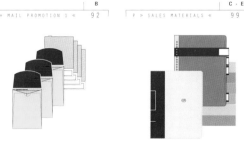

INTRODUCTION   SELECTED PROJECTS

COTTONG & TANIGUCHI
LANDSCAPE ARCHITECTS

C   D

E

COTTONG & TANIGUCHI
» ID AND PROMO MATERIALS «   94

TOLLES **soak** svansh **rinse spin**

PUBLICATION
FOX RIVER PAPER COMPANY

1994

PEPAR BY

HYPOTHESIS:

{ IF VARIABLES *f, o,* AND *x* RESPECTIVELY REPRESENT ANNUAL REPORT DESIGN FACTORS OF [1]UNIQUE COLOR APPEARANCE, [2]ECOLOGICAL RESPONSIBILITY, AND [3]PRINT PERFORMANCE, [(*f= 1, o= 2, x= 3*)] THEN PRECISE PAPER ENGINEERING UNDER CONTROLLED CONDITIONS (*1, 2, 3*) SHOULD OBTAIN AN OPTIMAL VISUAL DYNAMIC WITH MEASURABLY SUPERIOR RESULTS. }

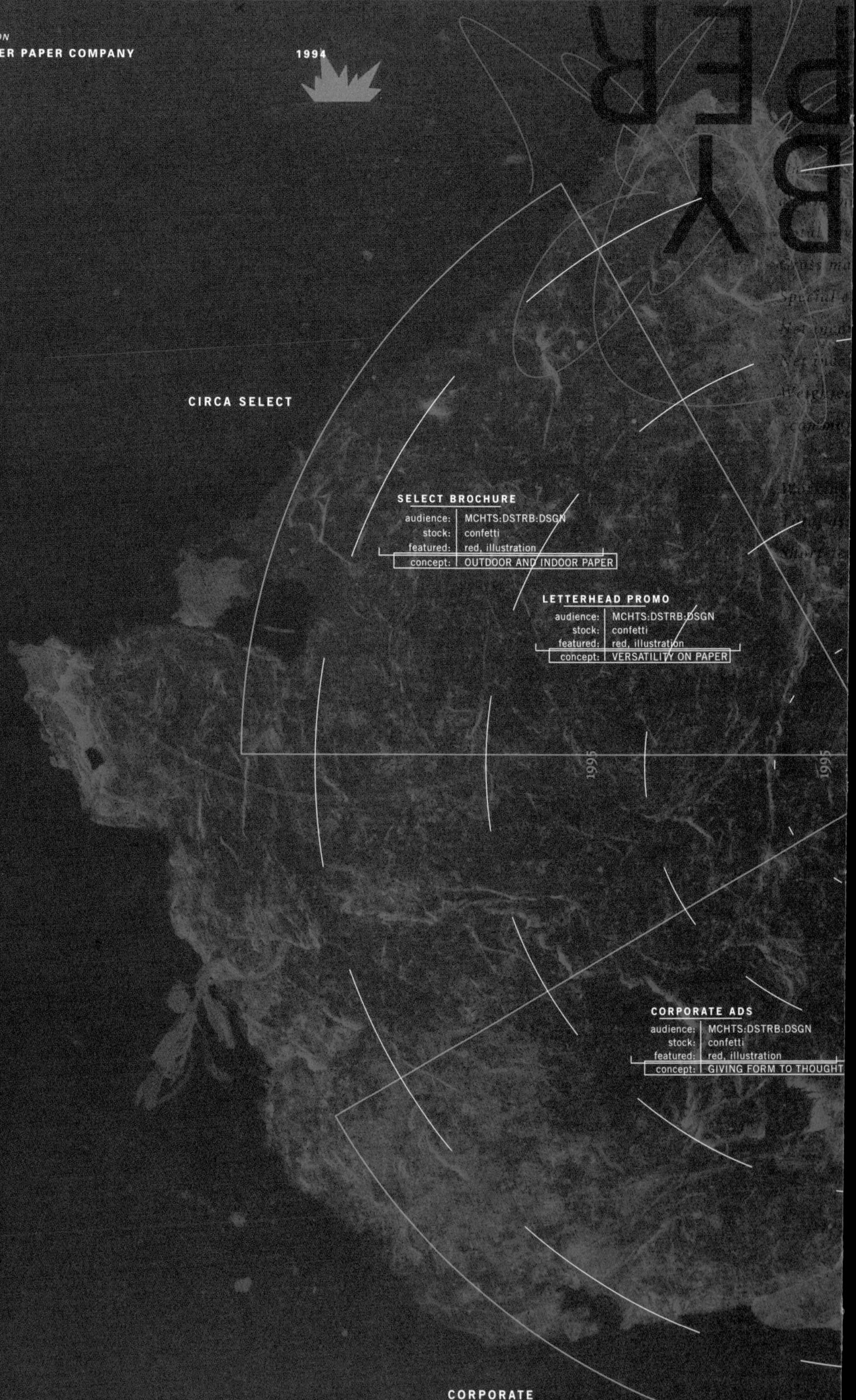

CIRCA SELECT

SELECT BROCHURE

audience:	MCHTS:DSTRB:DSGN
stock:	confetti
featured:	red, illustration
concept:	OUTDOOR AND INDOOR PAPER

LETTERHEAD PROMO

audience:	MCHTS:DSTRB:DSGN
stock:	confetti
featured:	red, illustration
concept:	VERSATILITY ON PAPER

CORPORATE ADS

audience:	MCHTS:DSTRB:DSGN
stock:	confetti
featured:	red, illustration
concept:	GIVING FORM TO THOUGHT

CORPORATE

Our relationship with Fox River Paper spanned a period of five years. It was a vital and interesting partnership. With Fox, we participated in the development of new papers, refined color palettes and redefined stocks in the current library as tastes changed over the years.

In our capacity as consultant, we were called upon to develop promotions that would introduce new papers or bring existing lines to the attention of the design community, Fox merchants and paper representatives. Sometimes these promotions related to the time of year when they were released (ie: a calendar at the new year, the Quarterly Reports promotion during annual report season) or they revolved around a recurring theme or event such as the Confetti Call for Entries series that consolidated work printed on Fox River Papers and submitted by the design community to the competition.

POSTER 2
audience: MCHTS:DSTRB:DSGN
stock: confetti
featured: red, illustration
concept: BIT PART #2

WINNERS PROMOTION #4
audience: MCHTS:DSTRB:DSGN
stock: confetti
featured: red, illustration
concept: WIT

POSTER 1
audience: MCHTS:DSTRB:DSGN
stock: confetti
featured: red, illustration
concept: BIT PART #1

WINNERS PROMOTION #3
audience: MCHTS:DSTRB:DSGN
stock: confetti
featured: red, illustration
concept: HELLO

WINNERS PROMOTION #2
audience: MCHTS:DSTRB:DSGN
stock: confetti
featured: red, illustration
concept: INTELLECT

WINNERS PROMOTION #1
audience: MCHTS:DSTRB:DSGN
stock: confetti
featured: red, illustration
concept: DIALECT

CALL FOR ENTRIES

SCHOOL TABLET
audience: MCHTS:DSTRB:DSGN
stock: confetti
featured: red, illustration
concept: WRITING THAT SOUNDS OUT

CONFETTI

OTIONAL BROCHURE
audience: MCHTS:DSTRB:DSGN
stock: confetti
featured: red, illustration
concept: RANDOM ORDER

CALENDAR
audience: MCHTS:DSTRB:DSGN
stock: confetti
featured: red, illustration
concept: TIME CAPSULE

QUARTERLIES
audience: MCH:S:DSTRB:DSGN
stock: confetti
featured: red, illustration
concept: REPORT ON STOCK

AR POSTER
audience: MCHTS:DSTRB:DSGN
stock: confetti
featured: red, illustration
concept: CONFETTI BITS

1995

PUBLICATION
FOX RIVER PAPER COMPANY   1994

In developing the concept behind the Confetti Fall Promotion of 1994, we identified several objectives that we hoped to achieve. We wanted to demonstrate a variety of printing techniques on the Confetti line of papers; we wanted to create a keepsake piece that designers would use daily; we also wanted to incorporate a sense of the global acceptance by designers for this collection of papers.

The idea of a desk calendar was not new, but it did accommodate our plan — it would be used daily as a reference tool and could be composed of a variety of Confetti stocks. By soliciting the participation of three other design firms located at the far corners of the globe — Turkey, Australia and Mexico — we also achieved an international atmosphere.

Each of the firms was responsible for a series of introductory pages that signaled a change in season. Our intent with these divisions was to create a sort of time capsule holding objects significant to the culture and place of their origin. Each capsule object represents a noteworthy element of human endeavor and experience in one of four general areas — science and technology, religion and philosophy, literature, art and music and daily life.

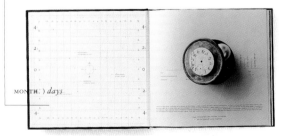

1. - *TOLLESON DESIGN*
    SAN FRANCISCO

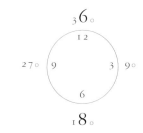

4. - *BÜLENT ERKMAN*
    ISTANBUL, TURKEY

3. - *FRONTEPIZIO*
    MEXICO, D.F., MEXICO

2. - *X + Y DESIGN*
    REDFERN NSW, AUSTRALIA

TIME BILL. WHO HAS T

MEAN TIME. ANYWHERE BUT N

SOLAR TIME. TIME MACHINE. TIME

MAKE T
TIME IS ON OUR S
TIME IS ELSEWHE
THE TIMES. BEHIND THE TIM

MAKE TI
TIMELESS. TIME HONOR
TIME IS ON OUR S
TELL TIME. WHO HAS T
THE TIMES. BEHIND THE TIM
NO TIME. ANYWHERE BUT N
TIMELESS. TIME HONOR

TELL TIME. WHO HAS TI

TIME CAPSULI

FATHER TIME. SIGN OF THE TIM

TIME IS ELSEWHE

TIME BILL. SOLAR TI

TIME IS ON OUR SI

MEAN TIME. ANYWHERE BUT NO

MAKE TI

S ELSEWHE

MAKE TI
ME IS ON OUR S
BEHIND THE TIM

TIME HONOR
IS ON OUR SI
WHO HAS TI
IS ON OUR SI
SIGN OF THE TIM
TIME IS ELSEWHI

TIME BI
TIME BILL. WHO HAS TI
WHO HAS TI
MEAN TIME. ANYWHERE BUT N
TIME IS ELSEWHE
SOLAR TIME. TIME MACHINE. TIME C

MAKE TIM

TIME IS ON OUR SI

THE TIMES. BEHIND THE TIM

TIMELESS. TIME HONOR

TELL TIME. WHO HAS TI

SUMMERTIME. FATHER TIME. SIGN OF THE TIM

TIME IS ELSEWHER

TIME BILL. WHO HAS TI
TIME IS ON OUR SI
MEAN
TIME IS ELSEWHE
EASTERN STANDARD TI

MAKE TIM

TIME IS ON OUR SI

THE TIMES. BEHIND THE TIM

TIMELESS. TIME HONOR

PUBLICATION
FOX RIVER PAPER COMPANY   1994

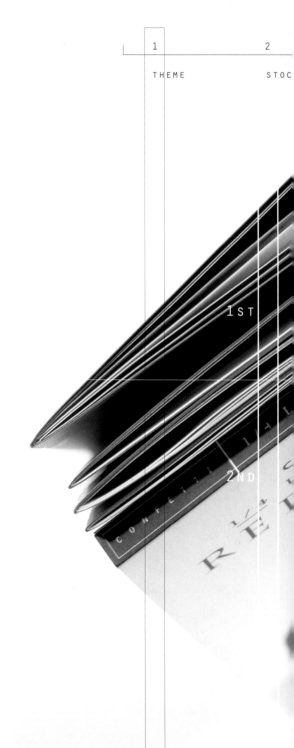

1   2

THEME   STOC

1ST

2ND

A quartet of booklets, each printed on different Confetti sheets and collectively titled 1/4ly Report on Stock, were produced around topics relating to the design and manufacturing of annual reports. An opening volume discusses the typical themes addressed in an annual; a second pamphlet examines efficient layouts for differently sized press sheets while punning on the selection of "stocks" the third evaluates the year in terms of black and white (photography) and contains a conversion table; and the fourth compendium examines charts and graphs and provides contact information for competitions judging annuals.

The foursome, collectively containing a large body of useful information that will be usable over the long term, were assembled into a slipcase so they could be kept as a reference tool.

2ND

3   4

B / W   NUMBERS

PUBLICATION
FOX RIVER PAPER COMPANY 1994

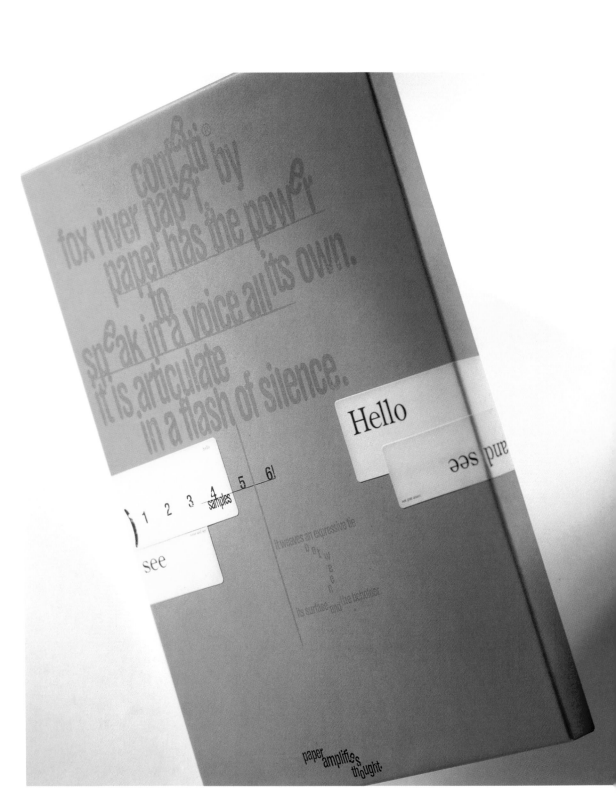

The Confetti Winner's Promotion packages were created as a vehicle to encourage a dialog between merchants and designers. From the Call for Entries, one designer from each quadrant of the country is chosen to participate in the promotion. The selected designers each create a piece on a theme established for that season's package (i.e. Hello, Wit, Intolerance, Dialog).

"Hello" evokes the days of our early training through simple "see and say" flashcards, fashioned to accommodate messages relating to the expression of thought on paper: "Paper has the power to speak in a voice all its own; it is articulate in a flash of silence."

"Four Views on Wit" proclaims: Wit is a diverse concept, synonymous with a multitude of ideas. In Old English, it meant to know or learn. As a noun, it signifies intelligence, astute judgment, ingenuity, as well as the five senses. In the plural, it connotes sanity, as: "keep your wits about you." And, of course, a wit describes someone who is humorlessly perceptive and articulate, skilled in the art of banter.

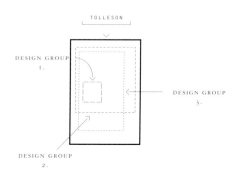

TOLLESON

DESIGN GROUP
1.

DESIGN GROUP
3.

DESIGN GROUP
2.

"Four views on Intolerance," covered with a stream of prejudiced assertions, makes a controversial social statement on its cover. From the Pharisees stoning of the adulteress to comments on more current issues including abortion, minorities and gay rights, Intolerance lands squarely "in your face" and beseeches you to open your mind.

The Dialect Promotion asks that we consider the different ways that a language is customized and fashioned to suit contemporary usage.

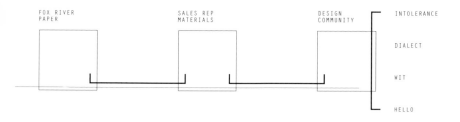

FOX RIVER
PAPER

SALES REP
MATERIALS

DESIGN
COMMUNITY

INTOLERANCE

DIALECT

WIT

HELLO

CALL FOR ENTRIES

FOX RIVER PAPER C<u>O</u>.
THE THIRD ANNUAL
DESIGNER COMPETITION.

The actor announces the Confetti Call for Entries in a play on the concept: "bit part". The "bits" are really the multi-colored content that are the basis of the Confetti sheet. The crowd is representative of the gathered masses who will flock to participate in this juried event.

1994

PUBLICATION
FOX RIVER PAPER COMPANY

N° 18

A poster announcing Confetti's new line of colors. The applied graphics discuss the color spectrum, environmental issues and Confetti's print performance in a scientific manner, substantiated by a diagrams on each topic.

PUBLICATION
FOX RIVER PAPER COMPANY

1994

N° 18

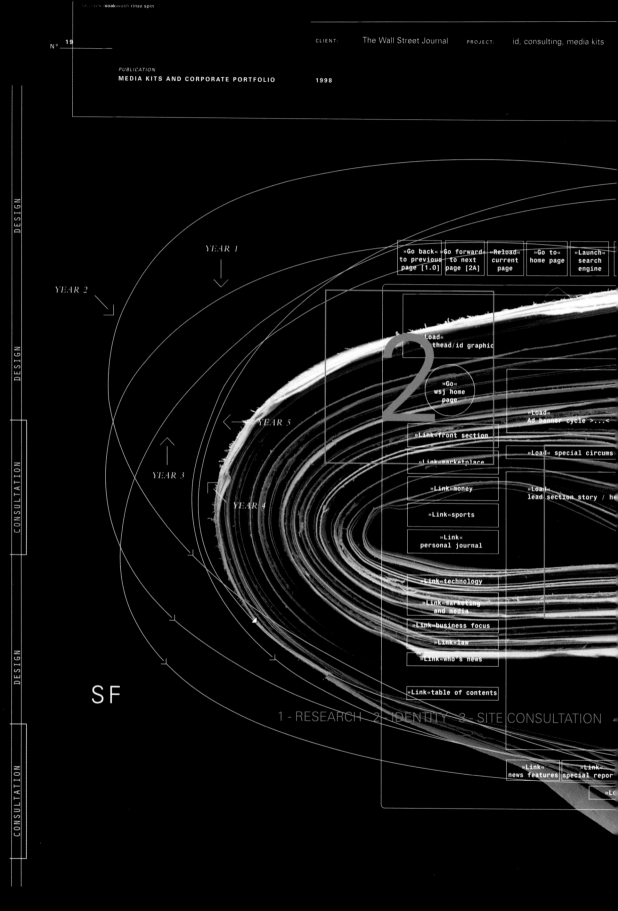

tou.sox soak wash rinse spin

CLIENT: The Wall Street Journal   PROJECT: id, consulting, media kits

PUBLICATION
MEDIA KITS AND CORPORATE PORTFOLIO   1998

DESIGN

DESIGN

CONSULTATION

DESIGN

CONSULTATION

YEAR 1

YEAR 2

YEAR 5

YEAR 3

YEAR 4

SF

2

»Go back«
to previous
page [1.0]

»Go forward«
to next
page [2A]

»Reload«
current
page

»Go to«
home page

»Launch«
search
engine

»Load«
thead/id graphic

»Go«
wsj home
page

»Load«
Ad banner cycle >...<

»Link«front section

»Load« special circums

»Link«marketplace

»Link«money

»Load«
lead section story / he

»Link«sports

»Link«
personal journal

»Link«technology

»Link«marketing
and media

»Link«business focus

»Link«law

»Link«who's news

»Link«table of contents

1 - RESEARCH 2 - IDENTITY 3 - SITE CONSULTATION

»Link«
news features

»Link«
special repor

»Lo

In order to help bring the Wall Street Journal online, a long distance collaboration with the Interactive Edition was established. The first step was to familiarize ourselves with the site's functionality, the content it would handle and the way the Interactive Edition intended it to operate.

Inaugural electronic versions of icons and buttons were passed from coast to coast so that artwork that had been finessed could be shared by both groups. Electronic comments were appended to the documents in word or sketch form and posted to a protected area on the internet.

NY

»Link«
all relative

»Print«
current
page

»Set up«
security

»Stop«
loading
next page

»Launch«
browser
home page

»Link«help

»Link«search

»Link«quotes

»Link«voices

ion head graphic >...<

4

3

»Load«
Alt ad >.1.<

»Load«
Story graphic

»Load«
Alt ad >.2.<

KIT 5 - MEDIA SALES/AD KITS

»Load«
Alt ad >.3.<

5

»Link«
sonal finance

»Link«
tools

»Link«
contact us

»Link«
your account

»Link«
advertisers

CLIENT: The Wall Street Journal   PROJECT: id, consulting, media kits

PUBLICATION
MEDIA KIT - 2ND EDITION

1998

PHS **2**

An understanding of all the components in the *Wall Street Journal* Interactive Edition Web site established a basis for the other elements that we created in support of the marketing effort. From the identity itself to the marketing collateral, the individual pieces all worked in support of the brand.

A suite of modular media/sales pieces to support the efforts of the marketing contingent was one of our first assignments under the new identity. The kits are constructed of materials evocative of the media, designed using typical filing hardware and formats. An undercurrent of traditional newsroom imagery serves as a bridge between the old and new mediums. In its second incarnation, the "new" media kit takes the folder idea in a new direction while retaining some of the file-drawer motifs in the diecut folder shapes and applied labels.

CLIENT: Leticia Trey Villegas   PROJECT: Intellectual Underground™ pha

PUBLICATION
**INTELLECTUAL UNDERGROUND
CONCEPT DEVELOPMENT AND PACKAGING
PHASE 1**

1993

EVIL

PAGE . *43*

0009

The Intellectual Underground is a community with a mind of its
own. A social system powered by the collective consciousness
of its members and defined by its own rights, symbols and
currency. The Intellectual Underground invites its global audience
to become I.U. citizens and stake their claim on the intellectual
landscape of the I.U. A journey to the Intellectual Underground
is the ultimate experience in mind travel; the only destination, a
place where reality is being reinvented.

The I.U. storyline is a classic tale of good vs. evil where the heroes
live underground within their own counterculture, while the corrupt
villains dwell in the upperworld in their strangely distorted reality.
Conspiracies, skirmishes, and intrigues abound in this environment
of blindingly clear rights and wrongs.

COLLABORATORS

A
CREATOR-PRODUCER
LETICIA TREY VILLEGAS

B
TOLLESON DESIGN

C
ILLUSTRATOR

D
AGENT

*THE DIAGRAM AT RIGHT REPRESENTS A VISUALIZATION OF AN IDEA AS IT FOR
THE ORIGINAL NARRATIVE, ENVIRONMENTS, CHARACTERS AND VISUAL LANGU
CHANGED DIRECTION WITH EVERY NEW CONTRIBUTION.*

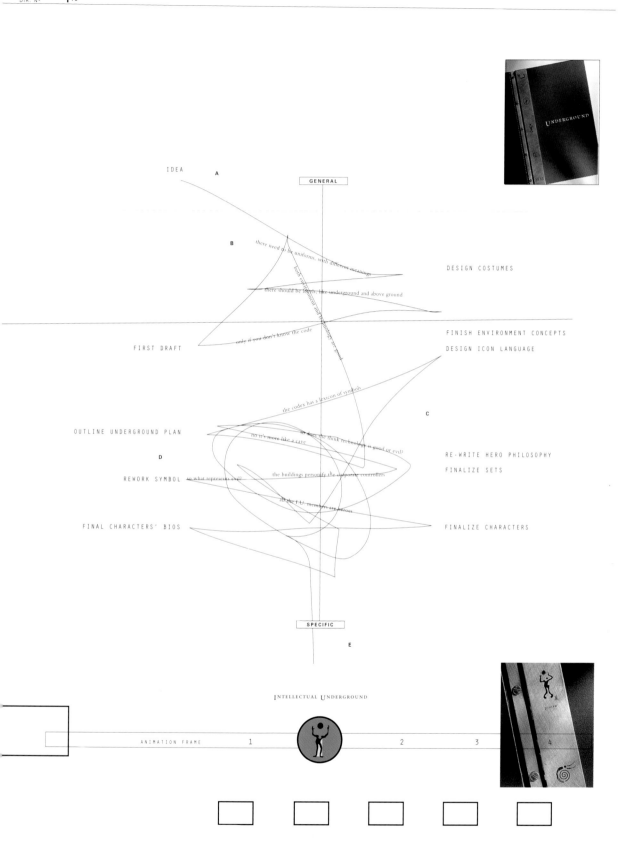

IDEA   A

GENERAL

B

there need to be uniforms, with different meanings

DESIGN COSTUMES

both costumes, like underground and above ground

only if you don't know the code

FINISH ENVIRONMENT CONCEPTS

FIRST DRAFT   DESIGN ICON LANGUAGE

the codex has a lexicon of symbols

OUTLINE UNDERGROUND PLAN   C

no it's more like a cave

D   RE-WRITE HERO PHILOSOPHY

REWORK SYMBOL *to what represents evil*   FINALIZE SETS

the buildings personify the corporate controllers

all the I.U. members are heroes

FINAL CHARACTERS' BIOS   FINALIZE CHARACTERS

SPECIFIC

E

INTELLECTUAL UNDERGROUND

ANIMATION FRAME   1   2   3   4

PUBLICATION
INTELLECTUAL UNDERGROUND   1993

GOOD

> I.U. CHARACTER

> I.U. ENVIRONMENT

> I.U. ENVIRONMENT

> I.U. CHARACTER

> I.U. CHARACTER

> I.U. ENVIRONMENT

1 - CAVE OF CONFUSION

The Intellectual Underground project was delivered to us in phase 1 of its development. The emerging ideas and metaphors continued to evolve until we finally closed the cover on the book six months later. A barrage of new ideas, character identities, and "what-if" scenarios came streaming at us daily while we strove to merge these embryonic, phase I elements into a cohesive product.

EVIL

 > I.U. ENVIRONMENT

 > I.U. ENVIRONMENT

 > I.U. CHARACTER

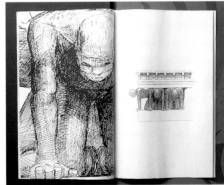 > I.U. ENVIRONMENT

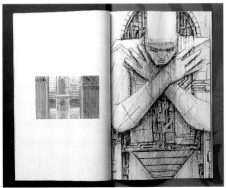 > I.U. ENVIRONMENT

 > I.U. ENVIRONMENT

PUBLICATION
INTELLECTUAL UNDERGROUND   1993

GOOD   EVIL

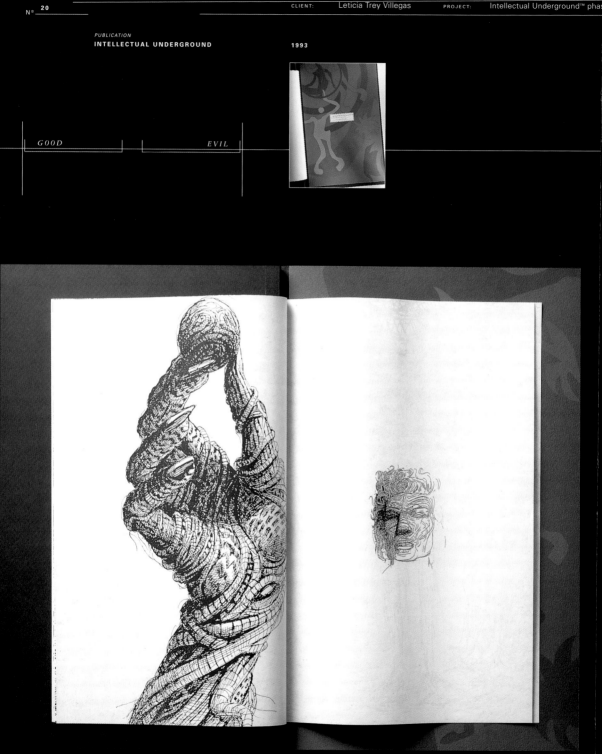

That product ultimately took the shape of a volume that told the story of the Intellectual Underground in words and pictures. Character animations and background scenery were invented to support the emerging story line. The book's intent to convey the basic plan and flavor of the production concept was ultimately presented to the entertainment industry.

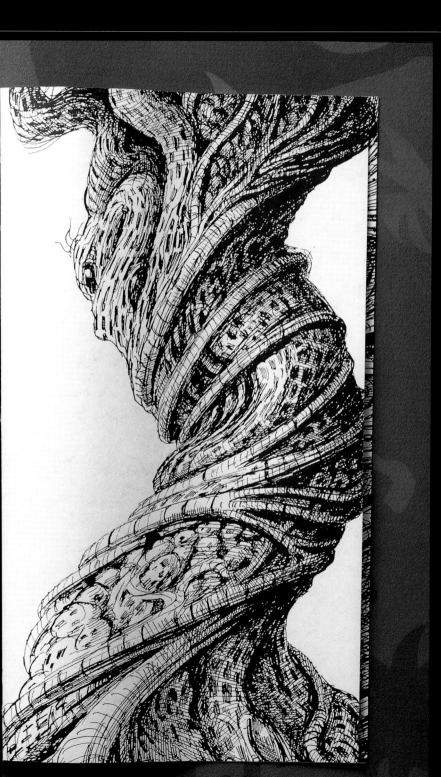

CLIENT: Leticia Trey Villegas   PROJECT: Intellectual Underground™ pha

PUBLICATION
INTELLECTUAL UNDERGROUND   1993

100
0
0

100
10
15
5

CLIENT: Alan Lithograph   PROJECT: id / capabilities materials

PUBLICATION
INSYNC.MEDIA SYMBOL DEVELOPMENT   1997

In 1997, when Alan Lithograph made the business decision to partner with Cal Litho and to create the new company, they decided to combine the identities of all three entities under the name of the new venture. So InSync.Media became the umbrella under which the capabilities of these separate concerns would operate.

The services the new company offers are all-encompassing in the area of digital media, pre-press and printing. In the print arena, Alan Litho caters to the sheet-fed market and Cal Litho fulfills high-speed Web needs. InSync provides advanced digital pre-press, supports its customers in an interactive media capacity and offers archival high-definition digital images.

The image for this multifaceted resource had to reflect all the component offerings and also have a good deal of longevity. Hence the identity studies include everything from printer's registration marks to screen captures in combination with a variety of typographic executions. The design that ultimately emerged is ecumenical in its affiliation — it speaks to the 2- and 3-dimensional products the companies market, and the typography tips its hat to their Web proficiency with the addition of "dot" between the components of the name.

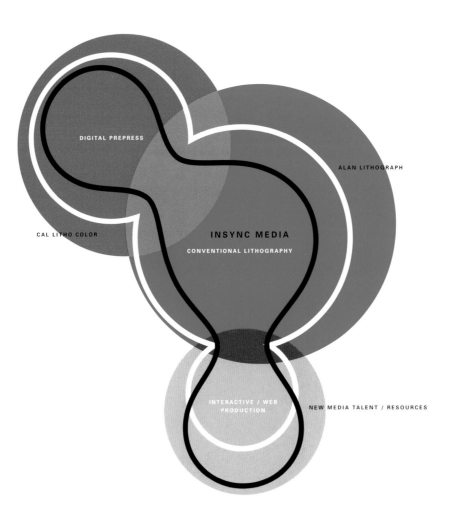

INSYNC.MEDIA

ınsync

insync

insync.

ınsync

insync.media

ıns s

ınsync.
media

INSYNMEDIA

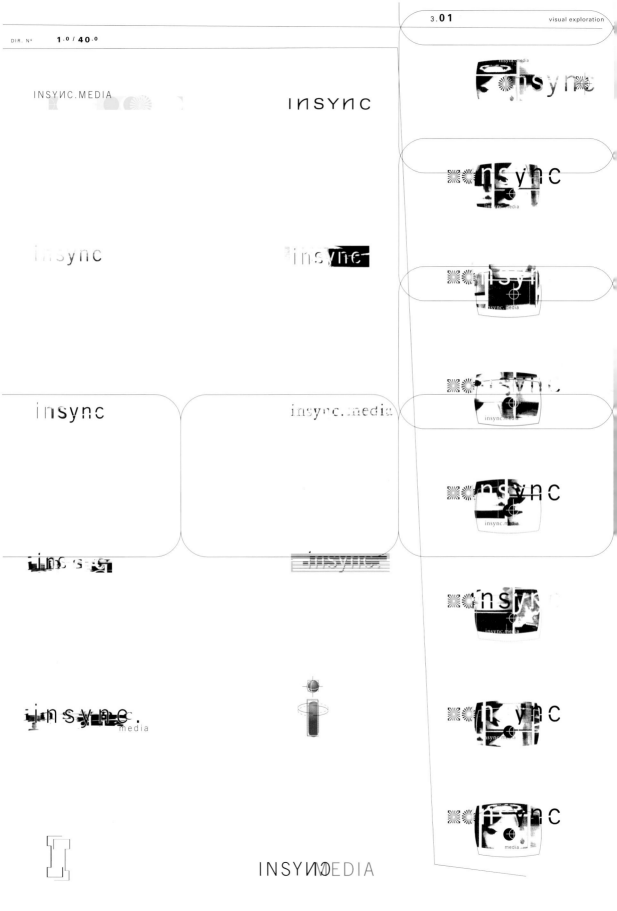

CLIENT: Alan Lithograph   PROJECT: id / capabilities materials

PUBLICATION
INSYNC.MEDIA MARKETING MATERIALS   1997

ALAN LITHO

CAL LITHO COLOR

INSYNC.MED

SYMBOL ART 1-C 2-C 4-C 6-C 72dpi 400dpi 800dpi
STANDARDS MANUAL

STATIONARY SYSTEM   PORTFOLIO
FAX ESTIMATE PROPOSAL CHECK TRANSMITTAL LABEL SET

MARKETING PROMOTIONS

MUG   HA

Having a printer as a client is rather handy. The items that the new venture would need to conduct business — cards, letterhead, brochures and the like — could be readily and lavishly produced; after all, the complexity and quality of their printed materials should reflect their expertise. The InSync.Media mark was ultimately carried forward into a multitude of 3-dimensional applications, including caps, trucks, building and event signage, even uniforms for the pressmen.

MOUSE PAD

TRUCKS

TRUCKS

SIGNAGE

EXTERNAL

INTERNAL

CLIENT: Kodak   PROJECT: package design / test marke

PUBLICATION
KODAK PROFESSIONAL FILM PACKAGING   1997

A > 1   2   3   4

✖

[A > 1 . 8]

In the spring of 1997, the New York office of Foot Cone & Belding asked Tolleson Design to take part in the exploration of packaging designs for a new Kodak product, Portra, a professional-level color negative portrait film, whose initial introduction would be into the South American and Canadian markets. The point of the study was to determine just how far Kodak could extend the reach of their brand identity by producing a range of designs that, at one extreme, included starving the package of most of the recognizable elements heretofore associated with the company.

>14   >15   >16

The chart on this page gauges the level of recognition that the various studies achieved through focus testing. In the strictest interpretation of the identity standards, the package sported solid panels of both Kodak red and Kodak yellow. Moving away from the mark were a series of designs that relied on an overall silver ink introduced to support the new brand; farther afield yet were packages completely wrapped in color portraits. Each version included the Kodak mark and the traditional red and yellow colors to a greater or lesser degree.

Our study's results produced a wrapper for a 5-pack of canisters that featured solid yellow, silver and black panels; a fourth panel was composed of a series of portraits — acknowledging the positive impact of all the brand criteria explored.

A

O

BRAND RECOGNITION : LOW

COLOR RECOGNITION : LOW

SOUTH AMERICA : PACKAGE TEST MARKET
PROFESSIONAL PORTRAIT FILM PACKAGE

PKG DSGN TEST N. : 1,2,3,4,5,6,7,8

C

Color negative film   >   ISO **400**   >   Pro-Pack   >   27° / E.I.400 / 5-IMA / 135-36   >   Color negative film   >   ISO

C > 1   2   3   4

20.⁰

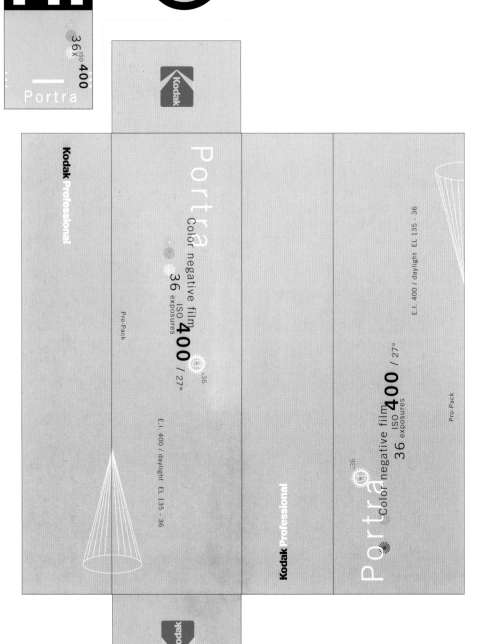

PUBLICATION

TEST 1 [A > 1 . 8]

CLIENT: Kodak

PROJECT: 5-pack, canister, can

DIR N° 2·0

BRAND RECOGNITION RESULT: 1 / PROFESSIONAL : 8

COLOR USE: LOW HIGH LESS MORE

To brand Portra, we introduced silver as the product color. As the film was to be marketed to professionals, this oblique reference to basic photo chemistry seemed a fitting solution.

A soft-focus portrait graced three of the faces of Test Package #4. When the package was constructed, the image was further abstracted, yielding panels that on quick inspection appeared predominantly yellow or red.

DIR. N° 5.6

CLIENT: Kodak

PROJECT: b-pack, canister, can

BRAND RECOGNITION RESULT: 2 / PROFESSIONAL VS. CONSUMER: 4

COLOR USE: LOW   HIGH   LESS   MORE

PUBLICATION
TEST 2

[B > 2 . 4]

portra

Color negative film / ISO **400** / 27° E.I. 400 5-IMA / 135 - **36** / Pro-Pack

portra

Kodak Professional

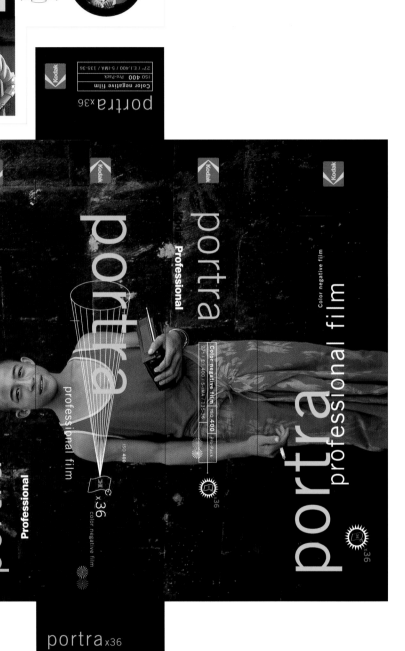

CLIENT: Kodak

PROJECT: 5-pack, canister, can

DIR. N° **10.0**

BRAND RECOGNITION RESULT: 7 / PROFESSIONAL VS. CONSUMER: 8

COLOR USE: LOW · · · HIGH · · · LESS · · · MORE

Test package #5 continued the march away from the elements of the established Kodak identity, featuring an image on all panels and only the corporate symbol to maintain a link back to the company.

DIR. N° **14.**0

CLIENT: Kodak

PROJECT: 5-pack, canister, can

PUBLICATION
TEST 4 [D > 5 . 4]

BRAND RECOGNITION RESULT: 5 / PROFESSIONAL VS. CONSUMER: 4
COLOR USE: LOW   HIGH   LESS   MORE

Retreating to a more substantially corporate position, this test package put forward a portrait overlaid with red and yellow logotypes. Small red and yellow panels also appeared on the short ends of the box.

CLIENT: Lam Research Corp.   PROJECT: capabilities and product inform⌐

PUBLICATION
LAM CORPORATE AND PRODUCT LITERATURE   1997

PALETTE OPTIONS

PHOTO : COLOR EXPLORATIONS
+ TYPOGRAPHY : COLOR VARIATIONS   / + PROCESS PATTERN INDICATION / + STEP KEY / + ICON
SIMPLE TO COMPLEX

cvd
DSM 9800 LP CVD

PALETTE OPTIONS

TYPOGRAPHY
COLOR
FORM
PHOTOGRAPHY

Lam Research Corporation makes machinery for the semiconductor industry. They engineer mechanical components that outfit the fab. In order to structure a meaningful system of product collateral for use by their sales force, we sought first to gain an in-depth understanding of the complex products and methodology employed in the semi-conductor industry.

TYPOGRAPHY	COLOR	GRAPHIC FORM PRODUCT SHAPE OR PROCESS REPRESENTATION	PHOTO PRODUCT OR PROCESS
GRAPHIC ID DEVICE ＞ A. PRODUCT GROUP ⌄	B.	C.	D.
tcp 1.	TCP 9100 TCP 9400SE TCP 9600SE	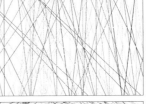	
etch 2.	R 4520 R 4520XL R 4420 R 4220XL R 4720		
cvd 3.	DSM 9800 DSM 9900		
alliance 4.	Multi-chamber processing platform	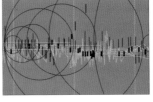	

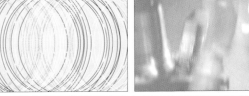

PHOTO : COLOR EXPLORATIONS
+ TYPOGRAPHY : COLOR VARIATIONS / + PROCESS PATTERN INDICATION / + STEP KEY / + ICON
SIMPLE TO COMPLEX

The organization of the resulting set of materials and how they were organized was directly influenced by the relationship of the processes that it is Lam's business to equip. Visual elements such as photography, typography, color, and graphic forms were each assigned a job in representing the content that comprised the brochures. The system is an intelligent and cohesive set of materials that can be applied to new products as markets open or Lam's capabilities expand.

An exploration of one cover demonstrates possibilities for the hierarchical relationship of information, depending on the required emphasis.

soak wash rinse **spin** ESON DESIGN

N° 23

CLIENT: Lam Research Corp.   PROJECT: capabilities and product informa

PUBLICATION
LAM CORPORATE AND PRODUCT LITERATURE   1997

HORIZONTAL
ORGANIZATION   >

PROCESS CATEGORIES

A high-level brochure is presented in three possible configurations and then included as part of a deeper product suite, demonstrating the design for a family of covers as it is worked out through the vertical parameters of the system.

DIR. Nº   **4**.⁰

VERTICAL
ORGANIZATION

EX.   EX.

PRODUCT GROUPS   PRODUCT GROUPS
1.   TCP   2.   ETCH
1.A SPECIFIC TCP PRODUCT   2.A SPECIFIC ETCH PRODUCT

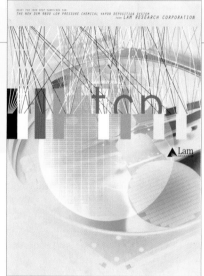

CLIENT: Elliott and Lucca   PROJECT: id / advertising

APPLICATION
ELLIOTT AND LUCCA LOGOTYPE DEVELOPMENT   1997

Since the company's inception, The Sak, purveyors of natural fiber handbags, had as their mascot a seated woman wearing nothing but her Sak bag. In 1997 they came to us, seeking to evolve the image of the Sak woman into something that would carry the brand into the next phase of its evolution. The new image was to roll out with the an advertising campaign carried by publications such as *W, Elle* and *Vogue*. The current line of Sak bags were largely hand-woven, textural, subtly-colored constructions — beautifully simple and straight forward, elegant in the purity of their form, evocative of other places and times. After consideration of several possible directions, we pursued an image-based solution that could elicit some of these same feelings through the physical form of the models.

The advertising campaign that ensued consists of images of the human body treated as a fixture — textured, decorated, flora and faunaed — made almost literally to resemble the product they carried. A group of women and men was painted in elaborate patterns, shrouded in yards of nubby fabric, caked with mud, masked by giant leaves or studded with thorns. Each is a unique creature that strikes a chord with the viewer. From the simple image of the seated woman with her handbag draped across her back, these new images helped the company shift the identity of the Sak woman to one of a complex, compelling and infinitely intriguing being.

phase I	branding	create new parent company logotype	merge existing sak women with new logotype	create and merge new division ids with existing logo and new parent id	organize hangtag system based on division identity
			establish parent, division hierarchy	establish division, product hierarchy	incorporate levels of company and product branding
				sak leather	sausalito monterey
				sak color	new color line for spring
				sak candy	preteen / high school
				sak japan	selected styles for asia intro
				sak accessories	belts, hats
				future products	luggage, men's
			retain existing sak symbol		

$\longrightarrow$

research	the industry	sak philosophy	product lines	products

phase II	advertising	media plan			
		photography review of 12 portfolios	develop multiple ad concepts		
			present 3 concept directions		
			1.	2.	3.
		photographer selected	the sak woman lifestyle one model / multiple locations	the sak woman in an environment one model / one location	the sak product form and texture several models / studio textures	concept direction selected

list of shots ———————— complete photography

Once this new image was in place, The Sak focused on introducing its brand across a broader product range;
an additional requirement to include the parent company, Elliott & Lucca, into the product identity also had to
be addressed. The ensuing studies show product tags that carry international city names in which the products
were marketed and the branding plan extends the collection to hats, socks, belts and other accessories that
were labeled with The Sak mark.

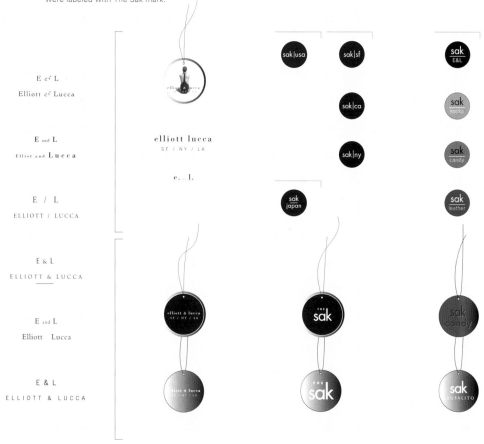

E c³ L
Elliott c³ Lucca

E and L
Elliot and Lucca

E / L
ELLIOTT / LUCCA

E & L
ELLIOTT & LUCCA

E and L
Elliott   Lucca

E & L
ELLIOTT & LUCCA

elliott lucca
SF / NY / LA

e. _ l.

parent sketches	elliott and lucca	sak branding	sak sub-branding

	E & L		SF		CANDY	SOCK
					COLOR	BELT
					SUGAR	SHOE
	LIMITED EDITION		USA NEW YORK TOKYO		CAP	SCARF

1   2   3   4

PUBLICATION
THE SAK ADVERTISING SERIES

MONTH **6** PLACEMENT **7.0** KEY V, M, G, E, TOL

MONTH **1**   PLACEMENT **1**.**0**   KEY **V, M, G, E, T&L**

CLIENT: Elliott and Lucca   PROJECT: id / advertising

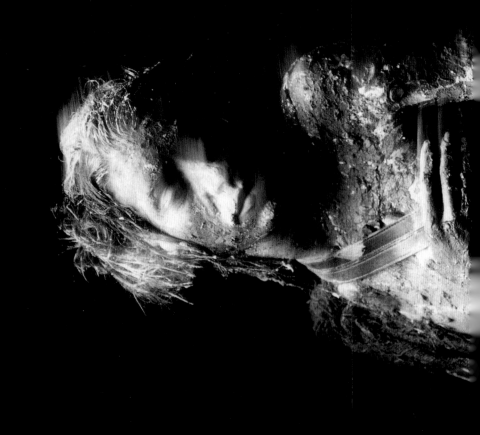

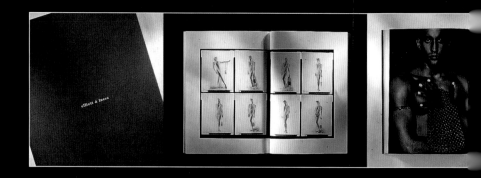

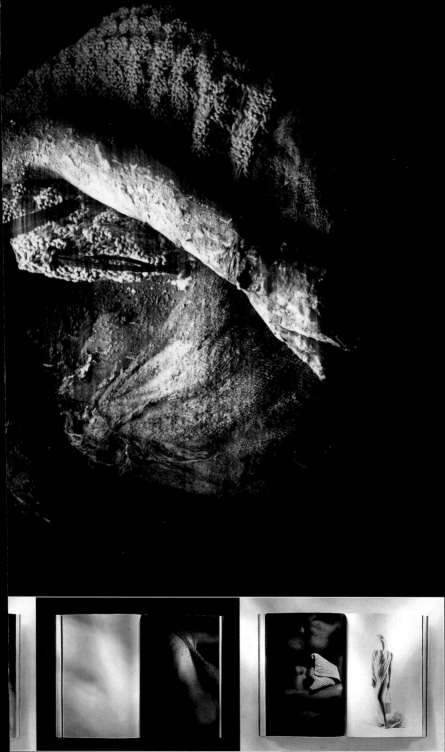

C NY

MP

ENLARGE NEWSSTAND PRESENCE

*STEVE, I'VE GOT A PROJECT FOR YOU. WE THINK WE CAN INCREASE NEWSSTAND SALES WITH A
COVER TREATMENT THAT DIFFERS FROM THE SUBSCRIPTION LOOK. WE CAN'T TOUCH THE
SPINE BUT WANT TO INVESTIGATE NEW MASTHEAD TREATMENTS AND COVER DESIGNS. I THINK
THE TYPE COULD BE MORE INTERESTING, TOO. IS THIS SOMETHING YOU CAN HELP US WITH?*

REDESIGN MASTHEAD

*WHAT WOULD YOU THINK IF WE WERE TO TAKE THIS A BIT FURTHER AND IMPLEMENT THE
FIRST YEAR'S COVERS FOR YOU — WOULD THAT BE OF INTEREST TO YOU? WE COULD
ESTABLISH THE VISUAL DIRECTION AND POTENTIALLY MODIFY OR ENHANCE THE ORIGINAL
CONCEPT BASED ON THE FEEDBACK YOU RECEIVE FROM THE PREMIER ISSUES.*

*GREAT. THAT WOULD BE IDEAL. WE CAN FINESSE THE NEW DIRECTION AS WE GO. WE'LL ASSESS
THE REACTION WE GET TO THE FIRST COUPLE OF ISSUES AND TAKE IT FROM THERE. LET'S GET
STARTED. I WANT YOU TO TRUST YOUR INSTINCTS — YOU ALREADY HAVE A GOOD IDEA OF WHAT
WOULD BE WELL RECEIVED BY THIS MARKET, I'M SURE.*

CONSTRAINTS

DESIGN

1

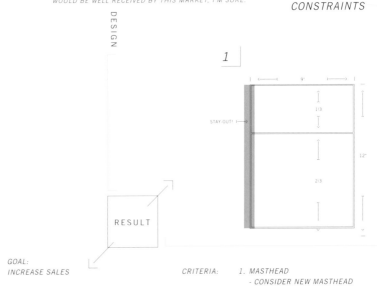

RESULT

GOAL:
INCREASE SALES

CRITERIA: 1. MASTHEAD
- CONSIDER NEW MASTHEAD
- MUST BE READABLE ON NEWSSTAND

Running along the bottom of the next pages are a sampling of cover designs.

EXP 01 - 1/42

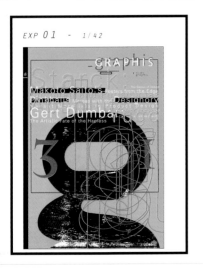

EXP 02 - 2/30

ST

ST

OF COURSE, MARTY, I UNDERSTAND THAT NEWSSTAND CONSTRAINTS DICTATE THAT ONLY THE TOP THIRD OF THE BOOK IS VISIBLE MOST OF THE TIME. THAT NECESSITATES A STRONG MASTHEAD DESIGN. WE'LL LOOK AT DIFFERENT TYPOGRAPHIC SOLUTIONS AND ALSO DIFFERENT WAYS TO HANDLE THE VISUAL IMAGERY. IT SEEMS TO ME THAT YOU WOULD BENEFIT FROM SOLUTIONS THAT REVEAL THE CONTENT OF THE ISSUES — SINCE YOU FEATURE TOPICS THAT RANGE FROM DESIGN TO ARCHITECTURE TO INDUSTRIAL DESIGN OR EVEN FEATURE ILLUSTRATION OR PHOTOGRAPHY, THESE COULD BE VERY RICH INDEED.

EXPERIMENT WITH COVER DESIGN

CREATE VARIATION

SOUNDS INTERESTING. CUSTOMIZING THE COVERS TO REFLECT THE CONTENT OF THE ISSUE SHOULD INCREASE NEWSSTAND SALES. WE WILL BE ABLE TO QUANTIFY THIS BASED ON SALES OF EACH ISSUE.

WHAT WOULD YOU THINK IF WE WERE TO TAKE THIS A BIT FURTHER AND IMPLEMENT THE FIRST YEAR'S COVERS FOR YOU — WOULD THAT BE OF INTEREST TO YOU? WE WOULD LIKE TO BE ABLE TO ESTABLISH THE VISUAL DIRECTION AND POTENTIALLY MODIFY OR ENHANCE THE ORIGINAL CONCEPT BASED ON THE FEEDBACK YOU RECEIVE FROM THE PREMIER ISSUES.

TYPOGRAPHIC SOLUTIONS

2

EXPERIMENT 01   EXPERIMENT 02   EXPERIMENT 03   EXPERIMENT 04   EXPERIMENT 05   EXPERIMENT 06

ISSUES 301 - 302 - 303 - 304 - 305 - 306

SALES

2. COVER
  - EXPLORE TYPOGRAPHIC COVER TREATMENTS
  - DO NOT TOUCH SPINE / SPINE HINGE

SALES:
QUANTIFY SALES OF FIRST TWO ISSUES
MODIFY DIRECTION BASED ON RESULTS

EXP 03 - 7/24

CLIENT: Graphis   PROJECT: cover series

PUBLICATION
MASTHEAD DEVELOPMENT   1997

While the in-depth study of the Graphis masthead yielded many interesting solutions, in the final analysis many of the explorations did not seem appropriate to the purpose at hand. Ultimately, we combined two classic fonts — Trajan and Syntax — to create a visual interpretation that had what it takes to endure. Even though several of the characters were re-drawn to enhance readability, the integrity of the typography is unmistakable.

1 2 3   4   5   6

EXP 03 CONT. - 7/24

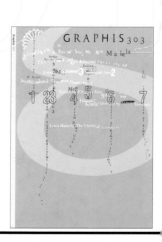

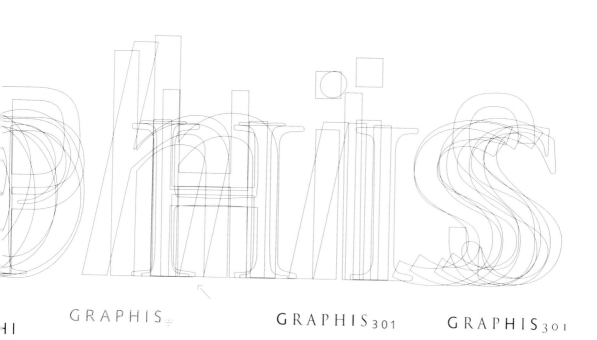

GRAPHIS

GRAPHIS 301

GRAPHIS 301

HI

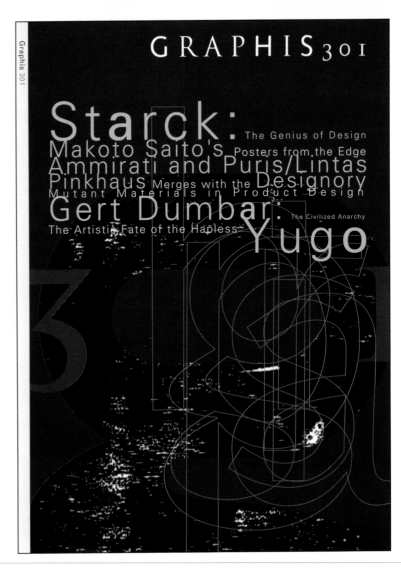

TOLLESON :soak:wash rinse spin

N° **25**

CLIENT: Graphis   PROJECT: covers

PUBLICATION
COVERS 1 AND 4   **1997**

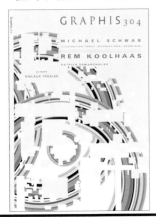

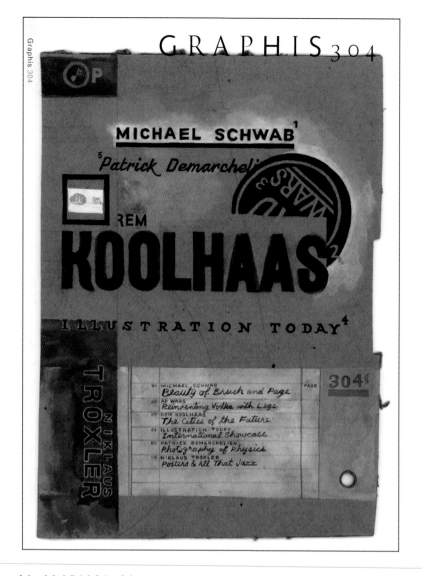

EXP *05* - *1/27*

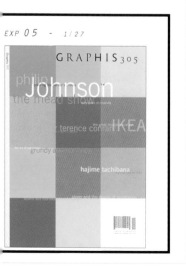

EXP *06* - *2/2*

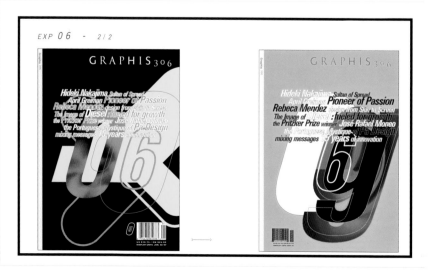

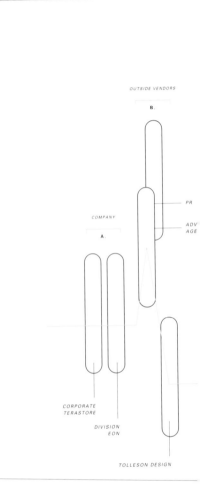

OUTSIDE VENDORS

B.

PR

COMPANY

ADV
AGE

A.

CORPORATE
TERASTORE

DIVISION
EON

TOLLESON DESIGN

TERASTORE IDENTITY DEVELOPMENT

PUBLICATION
EON IDENTITY DEVELOPMENT

1998

Hodskins, Simone & Searls hired Tolleson Design in Spring 1998 to work on the TeraStor account. TeraStor develops data storage media and optical readers. Their newest product, Eon, featured a dual-sided disk that could be read simultaneously by two laser-driven heads. This new technology promised to be many times faster than any other existing system in its ability to pinpoint information.

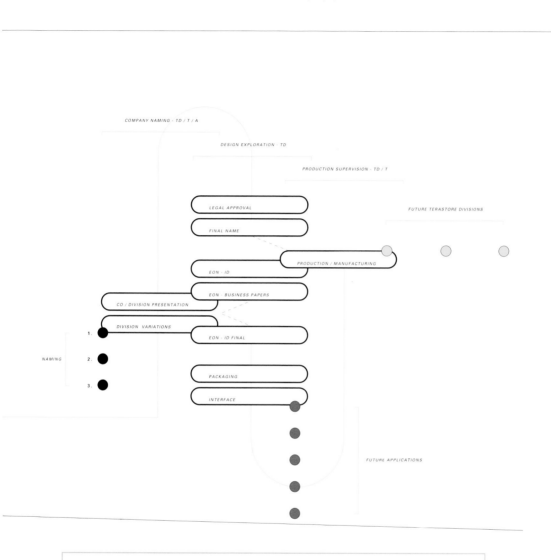

COMPANY NAMING · TD / T / A

DESIGN EXPLORATION · TD

PRODUCTION SUPERVISION · TD / T

LEGAL APPROVAL

FINAL NAME

FUTURE TERASTORE DIVISIONS

PRODUCTION / MANUFACTURING

EON · ID

EON · BUSINESS PAPERS

CO / DIVISION PRESENTATION

DIVISION · VARIATIONS

1.

EON · ID FINAL

NAMING   2.

3.

PACKAGING

INTERFACE

FUTURE APPLICATIONS

OUR TECHNOLOGY DEVELOPMENT PROCESS THE PROCESS DIAGRAM ABOVE ILLUSTATES THE PHASES OF THE EON NAMING AND IDENTITY PROJECT. THIS IS A TYPICAL SET OF PARTICIPANTS AND STEPS FOR THIS TYPE OF ASSIGNMENT.

Initially called to participate in product naming and to develop a symbol that could be branded onto the device, we were able to map out additional applications for the new identity.

APPLICATION
SYMBOL DEVELOPMENT   1997

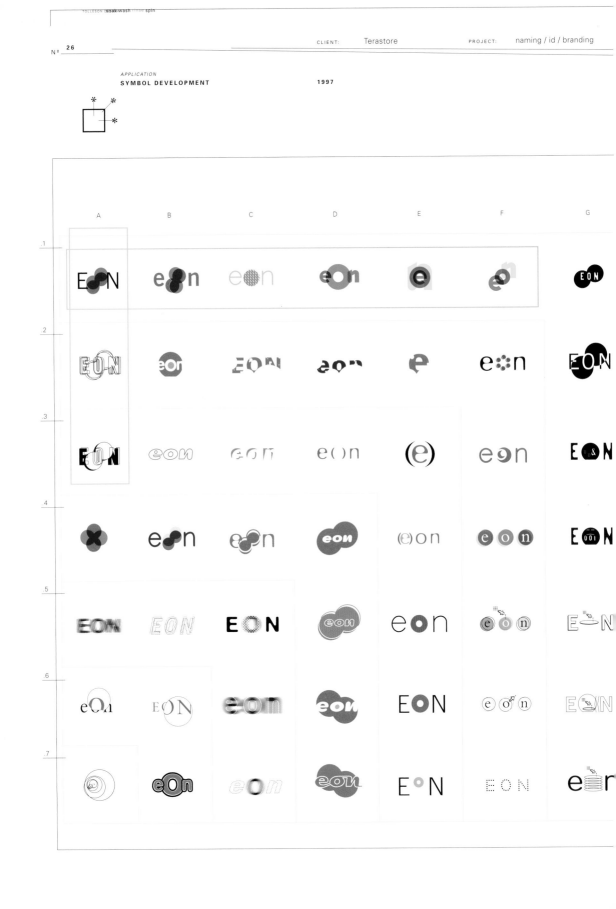

Multiple product characteristics influenced the design of the Eon mark. The capability to access two-sides of a disk simultaneously, to read with laser accuracy, and to seek information at speeds faster than previously possible each suggested attributes that could build upon one another to form a complex visual label for the product. One trait or another dominates in each of the representations below, depending on the treatment afforded the letter forms.

.1 - .8

The selected version of the symbol is derived from the software's ability to "see double"; it invites you to take a second look and reconcile the multiple images. Once this solution emerged from a group of over 200 studies, the final Eon mark then underwent further scrutiny into the subtleties of the characters and forms.

CLIENT: Terastore

PROJECT: naming / id / branding

APPLICATION
SYMBOL DEVELOPMENT

1997

EON .1

EON .2

EON .3

EON .4

EON .5

EON .6

EON .7

EON .8

EON .9

EON .10

A final study of the relationship of figure/ground, color and line weight allowed us to arrive at the final version of the logotype.

APPLICATION
OLD NAVY HANGTAG DEVELOPMENT   1997

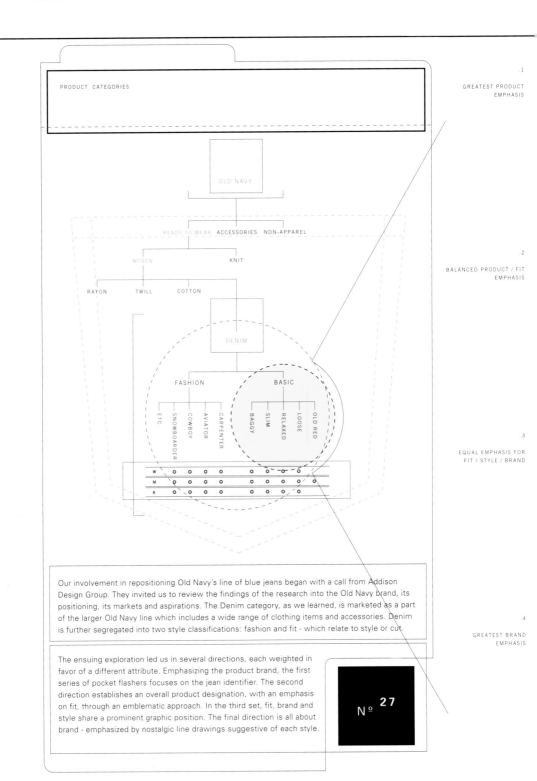

PRODUCT CATEGORIES

.1
GREATEST PRODUCT
EMPHASIS

.2
BALANCED PRODUCT / FIT
EMPHASIS

.3
EQUAL EMPHASIS FOR
FIT / STYLE / BRAND

.4
GREATEST BRAND
EMPHASIS

Our involvement in repositioning Old Navy's line of blue jeans began with a call from Addison Design Group. They invited us to review the findings of the research into the Old Navy brand, its positioning, its markets and aspirations. The Denim category, as we learned, is marketed as a part of the larger Old Navy line which includes a wide range of clothing items and accessories. Denim is further segregated into two style classifications: fashion and fit - which relate to style or cut.

The ensuing exploration led us in several directions, each weighted in favor of a different attribute. Emphasizing the product brand, the first series of pocket flashers focuses on the jean identifier. The second direction establishes an overall product designation, with an emphasis on fit, through an emblematic approach. In the third set, fit, brand and style share a prominent graphic position. The final direction is all about brand - emphasized by nostalgic line drawings suggestive of each style.

Nº 27

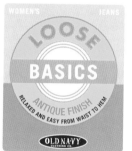

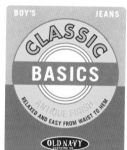

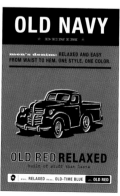

APPLICATION
OLD NAVY HANGTAG DEVELOPMENT   1997

OLD NAVY

BAGGY men

A COMFORTABLE FIT, PERFECT FOR LOUNGING OR ROAMING THE TOWN. BAGGY THROUGH THE THIGH WITH PLENTY OF ROOM FROM THE WAIST ON DOWN TO THE HEM.

fit MEN'S BAGGY   finish STONEWASH   d. BASICS

The final version gives equal consideration to all of these elements, with the design striking a balance between brand significance, product personality and the identification of the garment fit.

Nº 27

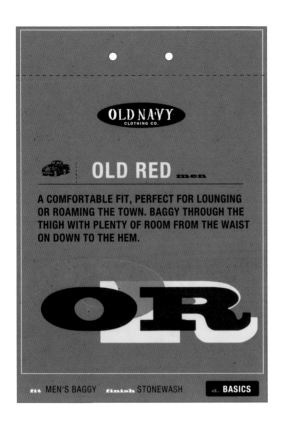

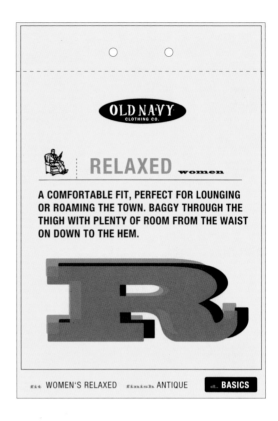

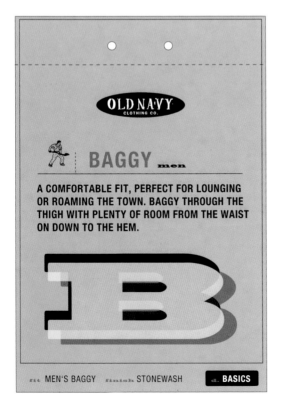

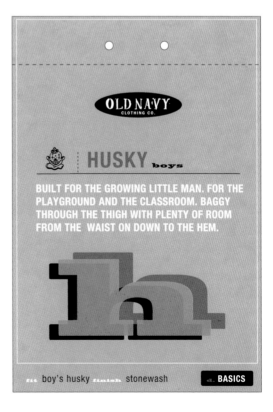

yeah...

yeah...

Cool man, nice project.
cool project.
yeah,

hey, that's plenty of time? 48 hours, that's a drag   yeah, that's a drag

yeah, we'll get it.
maybe

sure, plenty of time

what can't we do in 48 hours?

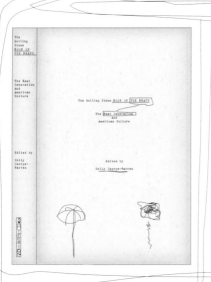

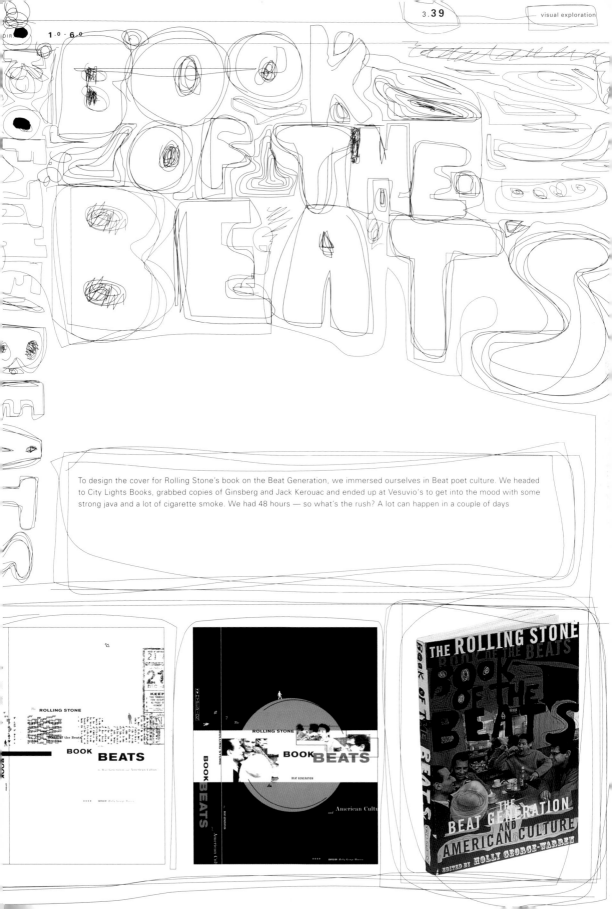

To design the cover for Rolling Stone's book on the Beat Generation, we immersed ourselves in Beat poet culture. We headed to City Lights Books, grabbed copies of Ginsberg and Jack Kerouac and ended up at Vesuvio's to get into the mood with some strong java and a lot of cigarette smoke. We had 48 hours — so what's the rush? A lot can happen in a couple of days

Plumtree Software's on-line indexing product was designed to categorically search and retrieve data from the Internet vis-à-vis an elaborate system of user-defined parameters and key word quests. Thus a multitude of data could be scanned daily and surveyed for relevance, then downloaded to a local server or workstation.

The analogy to a library card catalog system seemed obvious to us. Once we'd followed the demo, we understood this software functioned in a fashion comparable to an "automated librarian." So the literal reference

to library cataloging tools became a natural metaphor for the look of Plumtree's business papers and sales literature.

Taking its direction from a publisher's mark or seal, the Plumtree logo also bears a relationship to the arboreal form in its name through the addition of a leaf motif. Aside from the selected mark, we also proposed a number of other symbols which suggested a more or less literal relationship between the initial letter form of the name and either an organic or a bookish reference.

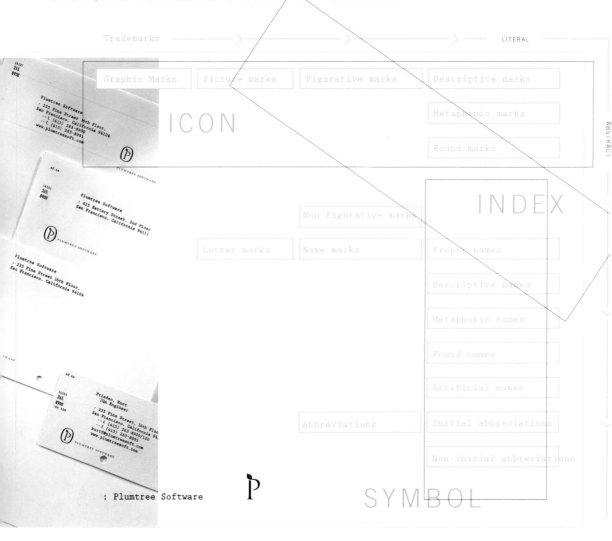

Trademarks — LITERAL

Graphic Marks | Picture marks | Figurative marks | Descriptive marks

ICON

Metaphoric marks

Found marks

ABSTRACT

INDEX

Non-figurative marks

Letter marks | Name marks | Proper names

Descriptive names

Metaphoric names

Found names

Artificial names

Abbreviations | Initial abbreviations

Non-initial abbreviations

: Plumtree Software

SYMBOL

CLIENT: Plumtree Software   PROJECT: id / marketing materials

FORMAL FEATURES

3D	FLAT
LITERAL	ABSTRACT
COLOR	MONOCHROME
EDITED	UNEDITED
DEFINED	AMBIGUOUS
AUDIBLE	SILENT

CONTENT FEATURES

POSSIBLE	IMPOSSIBLE
PLAUSIBLE	IMPLAUSIBLE
FAMILIAR	UNFAMILIAR
CURRENT	DISTANT IN TIME
LOCAL	DISTANT IN SPACE

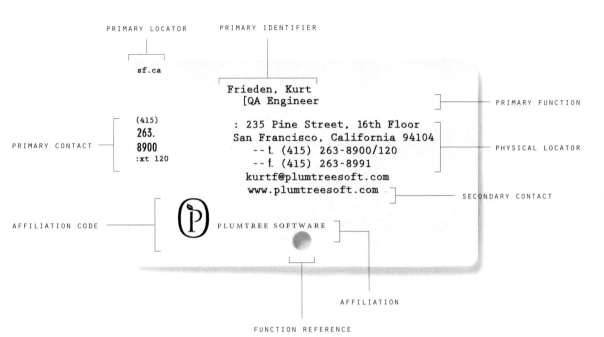

PRIMARY LOCATOR

PRIMARY IDENTIFIER

sf.ca

**Frieden, Kurt
[QA Engineer**

PRIMARY FUNCTION

PRIMARY CONTACT

(415)
263.
8900
:xt 120

: 235 Pine Street, 16th Floor
San Francisco, California 94104
-- t. (415) 263-8900/120
-- f. (415) 263-8991
kurtf@plumtreesoft.com
www.plumtreesoft.com

PHYSICAL LOCATOR

SECONDARY CONTACT

AFFILIATION CODE

PLUMTREE SOFTWARE

AFFILIATION

FUNCTION REFERENCE

P

concept ——————— object

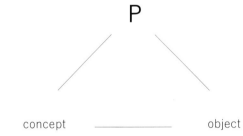

PUBLICATION
WOODTECH SALES PORTFOLIO   1996

When we first encountered Woodtech, they were a fledgling furniture manufacture
in need of just about everything to help them begin marketing their products.
In getting to know them, we were also introduced to their product lines (seven
at the time), materials and color palettes. Armed with this set of tools, we
embarked upon the development of a sales and design planning kit that
included everything from a sketch pad to detailed dimensional illustrations of
their furnishings to a container to display wood samples and finishes.

Employing metaphors borrowed from the industry, the Woodtech symbol came
to feel like a "brand" that had been burned into a surface; we eventually created
a plaque carrying the emblem so the identity could be branded" into the drawers
"of chests or beneath the seats of chairs. Many of the analogies active in the
Woodtech system — the routered notch in the business card and file folders,
the substantial boards and papers that make up the palette of printed materials —
were originally inspired by the Woodtech products themselves.

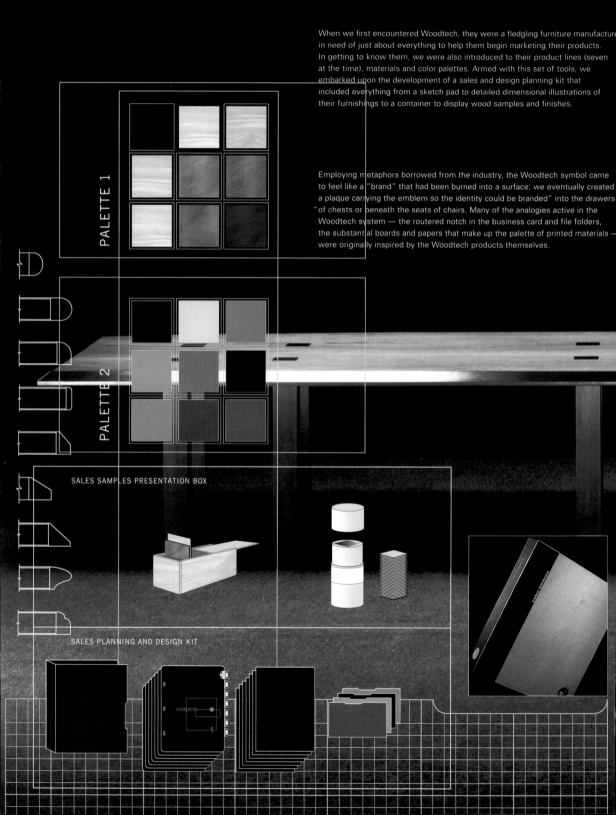

PALETTE 1

PALETTE 2

SALES SAMPLES PRESENTATION BOX

SALES PLANNING AND DESIGN KIT

Originally, the four founding members of Speck Product Design wanted their image to illustrate the way they viewed their relative positions within the company; they also wanted to point to their company name through a set of symbols that depicted small yet powerful objects.

N° **31**

CLIENT: Speck Product Design   PROJECT: id

APPLICATION
INDUSTRIAL DESIGN GROUP IDENTITY   **1996**

Once the design idea was established, each partner identified an icon that would best represent their contribution to the business.

(IDEA) story, 1   [symbol] FLEA

[Person] D A, C, L, Y, etc.

The tiny flea on one business card isn't an obvious fit until you learn that it can leap 350 times its own length; similarly, the ant can bear 80 times its own weight. The seedling sprout was selected for its allusion to potential/fertility and the atom stood for the building block of the universe, the smallest known particle of matter (at that time). In time, added to the flea, ant, seedling and atom were a robot, magic lamp, water droplet, molecule, gear, toolbox, puzzle piece frog and nut — each in his own way contributing to the mix and enhancing the group's capabilities as the company grew.

The company views its work as a scientific endeavor in which research is conducted, hypotheses are generated, options tested and measurable results achieved. Hence a parallel to scientific notation in the structure of the business system seemed fitting. The straight-forward, regulated character of the typography and an allusion to mathematical notation all contribute to the sense of precision and investigation. Even the color palette is evocative of the cool greens of test-tube glass and the vivid red of microbes as they're scrutinized under the microscope.

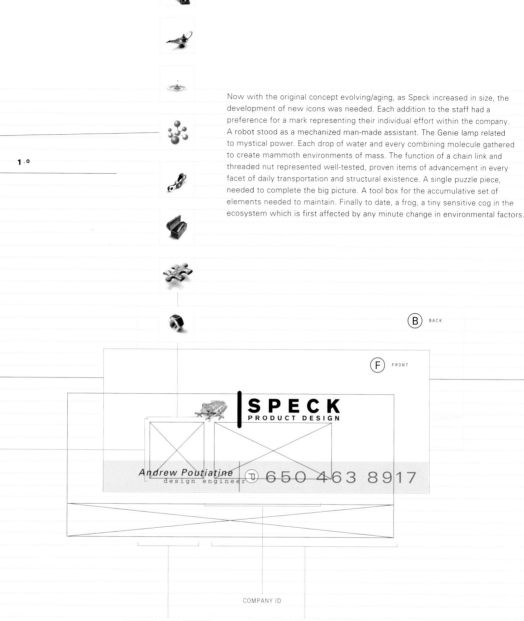

DIR. N°   **1**.0

Now with the original concept evolving/aging, as Speck increased in size, the development of new icons was needed. Each addition to the staff had a preference for a mark representing their individual effort within the company. A robot stood as a mechanized man-made assistant. The Genie lamp related to mystical power. Each drop of water and every combining molecule gathered to create mammoth environments of mass. The function of a chain link and threaded nut represented well-tested, proven items of advancement in every facet of daily transportation and structural existence. A single puzzle piece, needed to complete the big picture. A tool box for the accumulative set of elements needed to maintain. Finally to date, a frog, a tiny sensitive cog in the ecosystem which is first affected by any minute change in environmental factors.

(B) BACK

(F) FRONT

SPECK
PRODUCT DESIGN

Andrew Poutiatine
design engineer (T) 650 463 8917

COMPANY ID

INDIVIDUAL / TITLE AND ICON   PREFERRED PRIMARY CONTACT INFO

APPLICATION
EFFECT ISSUES

CLIENT: Effect Foundation   PROJECT: Identity

1993

child advocacy   illite
human rights

The charter of the Effect Foundation is to invoke change — in the role of catalyst, this charitable organization seeks to change the world for the better. The Effect name and identity imply the way in which a little change can produce a profound effect. An illustration is printed across the back of four business cards with the word *EFFECT* embossed on each quadrant.

The unprinted wordmark takes on a visually distinct character depending upon where it falls within each section of the drawing. Re-arranging the quartered illustration, also, contributes to the atmosphere of change, actively demonstrating the degree to which a small alteration can affect a perceptible difference.

3.47   visual exploration

unemployment

over-population

environmental degradation

EFFECT

free speech

racial discrimination

social change

EFFECT

Leticia Villegas

44 montgomery street suite 500 san francisco, ca. 94104
telephone 415 955 2678   facsimile 415 397 3309

global community

drug abuse

mental illness

FLIPSIDE LOGOTYPE SKETCHES   1998

Playing with all the visual imagery that the name, Flipside, conjures — upside down, inside out, through the looking glass, behind the curtain, hide and seek, changing places, opposites attracting — made the task of developing a mark for this video editing service more of a game than a challenge. Turning the concept this way and that, looking at it from new angles was the impetus to this far-reaching series of solutions.

 OR  OR

OR  OR  OR

OR 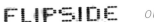 OR  OR

OR  OR  OR

PROJECT: id / animation / print applications

CLIENT: Flipside Editing

As can happen, the solution that the client responded to and our favorite were not the same. So, we evolved a number of versions of each of our two picks to arrive at the final mark.

FLIPSIDE
E D I T O R I A L

WARNING: BURST

MARS ATTACKS

NUMBER 01

1...discover life on Mars
2...learn Martianese
3...enjoy sex experiments
4...suspicious of heat
5...loot the headshop
6...burst

burst

A DIVISION OF VIRGIN INTERACTIVE

V

(1) **MARS ATTACKS**

NUMBER 01

1...unaware of martians intent
2...big laser pointed at earth
3...enjoy sex experiments
4...suspicious of heat
5...smile
6...burst

$2\frac{1}{3}$

$1\frac{3}{4}$

(2) **HUMAN CANON**

NUMBER 02

1...set sights
2...prepare landing
3...pack gunpowder
4...squeeze in
5...light fuse
6...burst

WARNING: BURST

HUMAN CANON

NUMBER 02

1...fail high school
2...join the circus
3...fail as knife thrower
4...ringmaster has idea
5...light fuse
6...burst

burst

A DIVISION OF VIRGIN INTERACTIVE

V

WARNING: BURST

BROKEN HEART

NUMBER 03

1...hire detective
2...tail lover
3...request photographs
4...rendezvous
5...clutch chest
6...burst

burst

A DIVISION OF VIRGIN INTERACTIVE

V

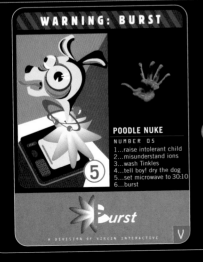

WARNING: BURST

POODLE NUKE

NUMBER 05

1...raise intolerant child
2...misunderstand ions
3...wash Tinkles
4...tell boy! dry the dog
5...set microwave to 30:10
6...burst

burst

A DIVISION OF VIRGIN INTERACTIVE

V

(5) **POODLE NUKE**

NUMBER 05

1...raise intolerant child
2...misunderstand science
3...wash poodle
4...tell child to dry dog
5...watch with amusement
6...burst

(6) **APPEASE GO**

NUMBER 06

1...select virgin
2...convince cause
3...climb volcano
4...(ceremony) sacrifice v
5...virgin? huh?
6...burst

SPECS
SIZE : 1 3/4 X 2 1/3
CARDS : 16
SERIES : 4
QUANTITY : 500

Burst, the in-house software development company within Virgin Interactive, arrived with their logo in hand and requested that it be applied to their marketing materials. In order to offer them the ability to customize their materials in as many ways as they have games, we came up with a series of sixteen different, witty interpretations of the company identity and applied these concepts to large stickers. The labels can be applied at random to any of the components of their marketing suite.

Since Burst's business focused on the creation of unusual games, and since games are fun, we decided to create a solution that was fun, too. The stickers shown here describe seven different sequences in which something "bursts."

BROKEN HEART
NUMBER 03

1...hire detective
2...tail lover
3...request photographs
4...rendezvous
5...clutch chest
6...burst

HOLLYWOOD
NUMBER 04

1...case the joint
2...fuel auto
3...commit crime
4...taunt law
5...go over cliff
6...burst

WARNING: BURST

HOLLYWOOD
NUMBER 04
1...scene 24 / take 3
2...make-up!
3...more fire this time
4...quiet on the set
5...lights... camera...
6...burst

Burst
A DIVISION OF VIRGIN INTERACTIVE

WARNING: BURST

APPEASE GOD
NUMBER 06
1...find and select virgin
2...convince cause
3...climb volcano
4...sacrifice virgin
5...virgin? huh?
6...burst

Burst
A DIVISION OF VIRGIN INTERACTIVE

WARNING: BURST

SIGHTING
NUMBER 07
1...plan trip to area 51
2...tighten nose implant
3...spot UFO
4...wave arms
5...take me to your leader
6...burst

Burst
A DIVISION OF VIRGIN INTERACTIVE

SIGHTING
NUMBER 07

1...plan trip to area 51
2...tighten nose implant
3...spot UFO
4...wave arms
5...take me to your leader
6...burst

APPLICATION
LANGUAGE INSTRUCTION SYMBOL   1994

Shortened from "Dynamic Education," DynEd is the producer of a unique Japanese/English and English/Japanese language training software. DynEd's learning system is responsive to an individual pupil's level of ability and the speed at which he/she assimilates new skills. Above all, DynEd wanted to convey the fact that the "teacherless" aspect of their method of language acquisition doesn't diminish the quality of the instruction. On the contrary, it allows the student to learn at a comfortable pace and to customize his training to meet individual requirements.

DynEd positioned themselves in the training market as publishers for a new age. The care and quality that was emblematic of DynEd's products struck us as comparable to the noble efforts of scholarly publishing houses, who have issued works for consumption by students throughout the history of learning. It seemed logical to pursue a mark for this educational firm that was evocative of the type of icon traditionally affixed to printed volumes.

The exploration of such a monogram produced a range of options. Of particular concern to DynEd, and another one of the reasons we were drawn to this solution, was the correct pronunciation of their name — Dyn Ed; not Dy Ned. They hoped that the visual rendering of their company name would lead the consumer to the conclusion that they were indeed a part of the educational services community.

PUBLICATION

thrill kill

1998

Satanic, demonic, even sadistic is the only way to describe the content of the game, Thrill Kill. To create a marketable presence for this package, we called upon our dark side to evoke an appropriately frightening image. To save yourself from a fate worse than death, you must escape the clutches of your pursuers. In keeping score, points are garnered for tortures inflicted rather than for the clean kill, with teammates ganging up to inflict greater pain on the weaker players. The tagline "this game is giving Satan nightmares" supports the icon which shows Satan surveying the scene from a safe distance — he doesn't dare participate.

APPLICATION
COCOBLISS PACKAGING   1992

Cocobliss. A boutique chocolatier brought us the assignment to name and brand their line of truffles and confections. After arriving at the name, the symbol of a heavenly herald came naturally enough — eventually evolving into signage, packaging and fixtures for the emporium of this storefront purveyor of high-quality chocolates.

CLIENT: Kinetics   PROJECT: id / collateral / interactive

PUBLICATIONS

KINETICS CORPORATE / SALES MATERIALS   1995 - 1999

During the course of our 5+ year relationship with Kinetics, we have been called upon to identify not only the parent company and to devise sales and marketing collateral addressing its various target markets, but also to develop independent identities for its many subsidiary companies. In defining the visual relationship between Kinetics and it divisions, we took our lead from the physical properties of the products they supply and the

delivery systems that carry these essential chemicals to fabrication facilities. Each piece of the system was influenced by a palette consisting of air, water, gas and stainless-steel pipe fittings. We reinvented this subject matter to suit each new communication vehicle required by the component interests while maintaining a consistent image – allowing the collection of literature to co-exist under the corporate umbrella.

CORPORATE IDENTITY
SUB-BRANDS
ICON VOCABULARY
DIVISIONAL IDENTITIES

SALES COLLATERAL
MARKETING COLLATERAL
CORPORATE CAPABILITIES BROCHURE
PRESENTATION MATERIALS

SIGNAGE
EXHIBIT GRAPHICS
VEHICLE IDENTIFICATION

ID.1   L.1/2   ID.2

IDENTITY SYSTEM

MARKETING COLLATERAL

PRODUCT INFORMATION

The intrinsic simplicity and graphic quality of these highly-refined industrial elements evolved to serve the messaging needs of the wide array of Kinetics sub-brands. From identity to sales materials to interactive communications, the range of images comprising the Kinetics visual system work to unify and identify its extensive offering of products and services.

HVAC

BIO/PHARM

INTERACTIVE DESIGN
SALES DEMO
WEB SITE

IN.1

USF

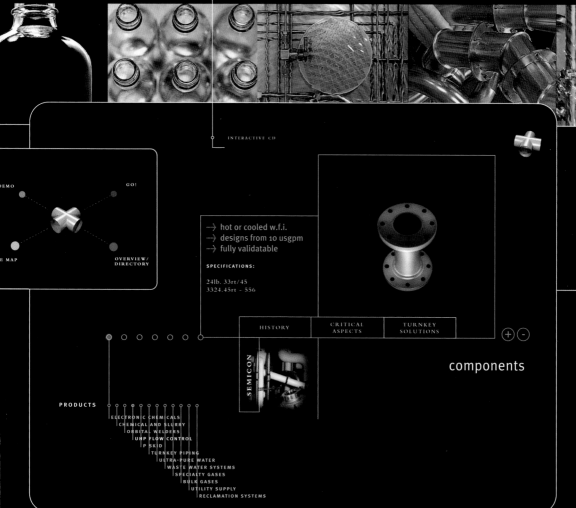

INTERACTIVE CD

DEMO   GO!

E MAP   OVERVIEW/
               DIRECTORY

----> hot or cooled w.f.i.
----> designs from 10 usgpm
----> fully validatable

SPECIFICATIONS:

24lb. 33rt/45
3324.45rt - 556

| HISTORY | CRITICAL ASPECTS | TURNKEY SOLUTIONS |

components

SEMICON

PRODUCTS

ELECTRONIC CHEMICALS
CHEMICAL AND SLURRY
ORBITAL WELDERS
UHP FLOW CONTROL
P SKID
TURNKEY PIPING
ULTRA-PURE WATER
WASTE WATER SYSTEMS
SPECIALTY GASES
BULK GASES
UTILITY SUPPLY
RECLAMATION SYSTEMS

CLIENT: Various   PROJECT: id

PUBLICATION
SYMBOLS AND LOGOTYPES   1992 - 1999

DIR. Nº   1.0 - 24

PILLAR

concept

LIZGOLF
BY LIZ CLAIBORNE

RI VEN
SEQUEL TO MYST

HE'D BEEN THINKING ABOUT
IT FOR WEEKS

HE'D BEEN THINKING ABOUT
IT FOR WEEKS

HE'D BEEN THINKING ABOUT
IT FOR WEEKS

HE'D BEEN THINKING ABOUT
IT FOR WEEKS

PUBLICATION
aka STOCK BOOK   1999

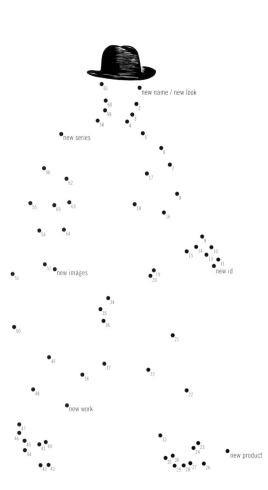

new name / new look

new series

new images

new id

new work

new product

NEW LOOK	NEW ID	NEW PRODUCT	NEW IMAGES	NEW SERIES
□=○	○○○			

In an effort to capture additional market share and reposition their offering, the stock image company Photonica launched the aka catalog. In affiliation with Photonica, aka includes a workhorse collection reaching for a broader appeal than its parent venture. The premier volume includes images in business categories — people, concepts and objects. The plan is to follow with a selection focused on sports. The images maintain the same quality and appeal that have garnered Photonica the reputation it currently enjoys, while allowing the Photonica name to seek a new height in the area of fine art imagery.

1   The small format of the aka catalog (one-half that of the current Photonica book) creates the feeling of a handbook, encouraging the practice of leaving it out on a desk, to be at-hand and usable as a reference book.

2 ⇨ The aka mark we developed, with its circular motifs, plays off the missing dots that should appear between each of the initials. The arrangement of the images in the archive tell subtle stories, reinforcing the "also known as" or dual identity concept — look again, the pairing of images is not always what it first appears.

LOGO STUDY:		REASON:		
		Type studies, graphic elements and patterns suggested for the aka brand revolve around a dot or a circular direction. Each serves to extend the visual reach of the aka (dot, dot, dot) logotype.		

TYPE STUDY:

SECTION:	DESIGN:	SECTION:	DESIGN:	
fig. *a*	CONCEPTS	fig. *d*	 CONCEPTS	
fig. *b*	OBJECTS	fig. *e*	OBJECTS	
fig. *c*	PEOPLE	fig. *f*	PEOPLE	

PATTERN STUDY:

SECTION:	DESIGN:	SECTION:	DESIGN:	
fig. *g*	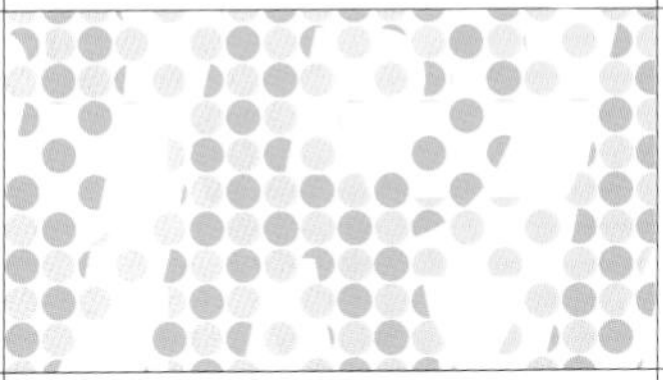	fig. *j*		
fig. *h*		fig. *k*		
fig. *i*		fig. *l*		

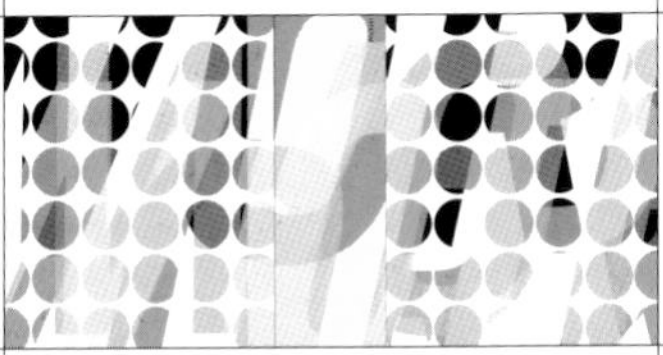

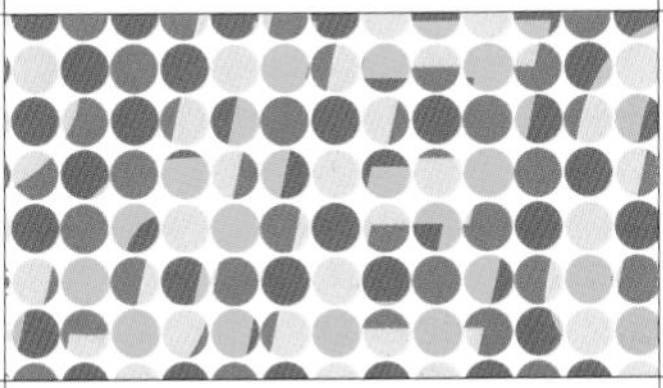

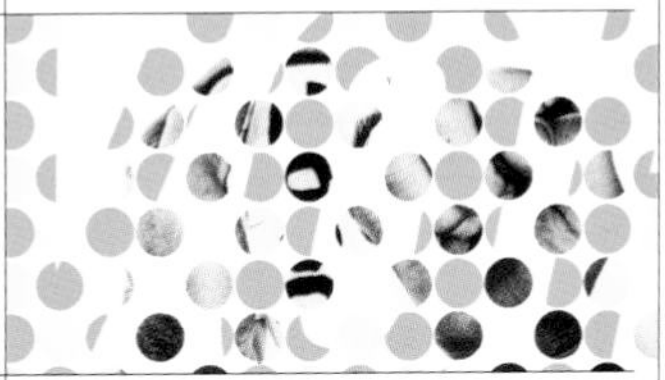

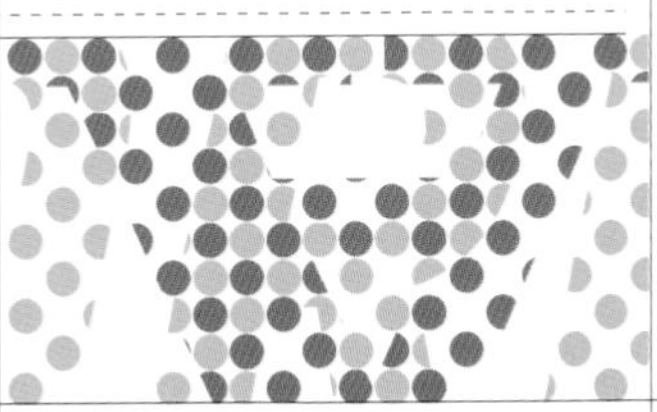

CLIENT: Photonica   PROJECT: id / promotion book

PUBLICATION
aka STOCK BOOK   **1999**

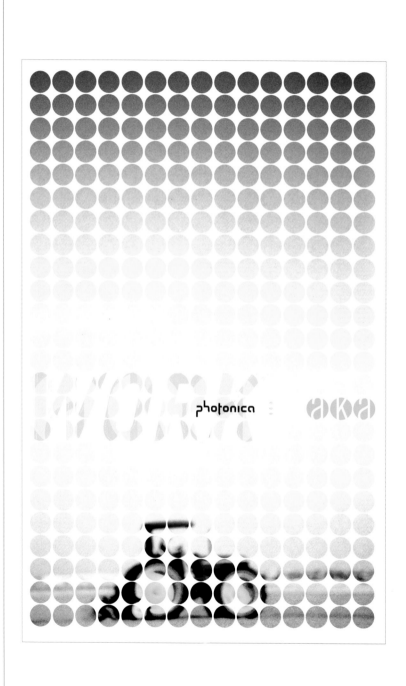

NO.**1**

⇨
⇨
⇨
⇨

photonica   aka

GRAPHIC: | **COVER**

REASON:

The images contained in
the aka resource aren't
always what they seem
The arrangement of ima
on any given page tell
multiple stories limited
by the viewer's imagina

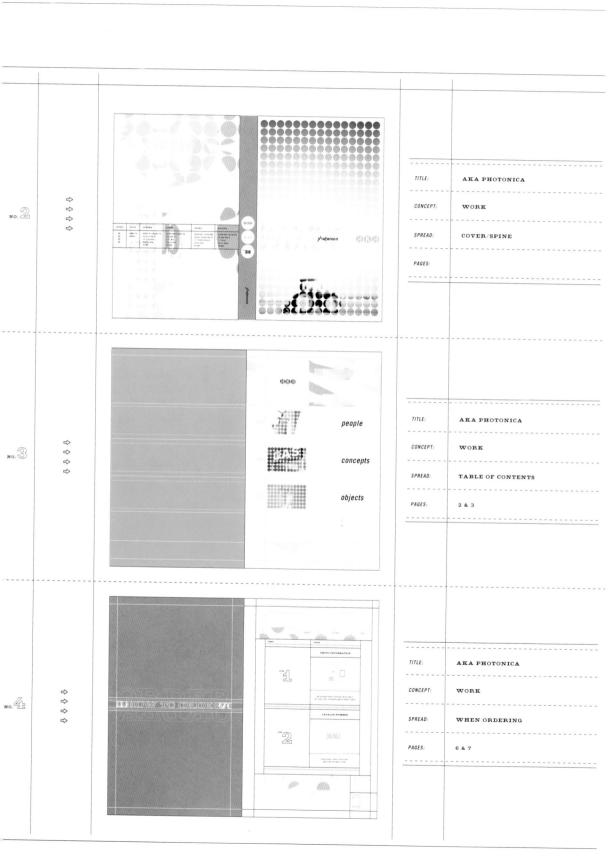

NO. 2

TITLE:	AKA PHOTONICA
CONCEPT:	WORK
SPREAD:	COVER/SPINE
PAGES:	

NO. 3

TITLE:	AKA PHOTONICA
CONCEPT:	WORK
SPREAD:	TABLE OF CONTENTS
PAGES:	2 & 3

NO. 4

TITLE:	AKA PHOTONICA
CONCEPT:	WORK
SPREAD:	WHEN ORDERING
PAGES:	6 & 7

PUBLICATION
aka STOCK BOOK   1999

<table>

	TITLE:	AKA PHOTONICA
	CONCEPT:	WORK
	CONTENT:	STOCK PHOTOGRAPHY
NO. 4	SECTION:	OBJECTS
	PAGES:	230 - 311
	SIZE:	5 13/16" X 9"
	LOCATION:	JAPAN, EUROPE, SPAIN, NORTH AMERICA

</table>

SUBJECTS: Globes Business: Enterprise & Occupations Cogs Writing: Pens Construction Decision Chance Landmarks Authority Dance Telecommunication Connections Outdoors Judgment Action Vision On the move Gardening Recreation Electricity Time Property Travel Communication Data Voice Equipment Gears Entertainment Relaxation Presentation Gambling Transportation Lifestyle Fashion Special Effects Direction Information Connections Outdoors Judgment Action Vision Domestic: Life & Leisure On the move Couples Architecture Globes Technology Collage Hands Brains X-rays Calendars Fish Coffee Emotion Transportation Commuting Signs Subways Freeways Helicopters Watches Keyboards Money Real Estate Piggy Banks Industry Landscape Agriculture Windmills Birds Gears On the road Bridges Trucks Trains Airplanes Airports Art Travel Elevators Safes Bathrooms Scales Gears Mousetraps Newspapers Driving Sports & Games Dice Dominoes Puzzles Golf Lakes Boating Horseback Riding Magnifying Glass Look/Listen Telecommunications Eyeglasses Fashion Travel

GAMES:

TITLE:	**AKA PHOTONICA**
CONCEPT:	**WORK**
SECTION:	**CONCEPTS**
PAGES:	**088 - 229**

SUBJECTS: Architecture Globes Technology Collage Hands Brains X-rays Calendars Fish Coffee Emotion Transportation Commuting Signs Subways Freeways Helicopters Watches Keyboards Money Real Estate Piggy Banks Industry Landscape Agriculture Windmills Birds Gears On the road Bridges Trucks Trains Airplanes Airports Art Travel Elevators Safes Bathrooms Scales Gears Mousetraps Newspapers Driving Sports & Games Dice Dominoes Puzzles Golf Lakes Boating Horseback Riding Magnifying Glass Look/Listen

GAMES: *SAMPLE*

TITLE:	**AKA PHOTONICA**
CONCEPT:	**WORK**
SECTION:	**PEOPLE**
PAGES:	**008 - 087**

SUBJECTS: Architecture Globes Technology Collage Hands Brains X-rays Calendars Fish Coffee Emotion Transportation Commuting Signs Subways Freeways Helicopters Watches Keyboards Money Real Estate Piggy Banks Industry Landscape Agriculture Windmills Birds Gears On the road Bridges Trucks Trains Airplanes Airports Art Travel Elevators Safes Bathrooms Scales Gears Mousetraps Newspapers Driving Sports & Games Dice Dominoes Puzzles Golf Lakes Boating Horseback Riding Magnifying Glass Look/Listen

GAMES: *SAMPLE*

TOLLES soak wash rinse spin

APPLICATION
DISNEY INTRANET SITE   **1996**

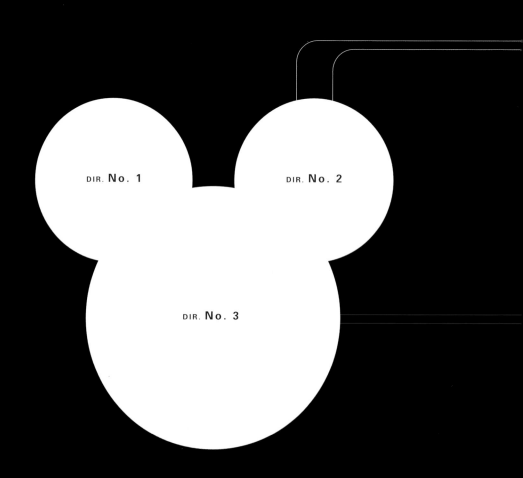

DIR. No. 1   DIR. No. 2

DIR. No. 3

In collaboration with Netscape, we worked to develop a graphic interface for the Disney intranet site, upon which would be housed the most up-to-date, classified and sensitive of internal communiques. To construct a system that served the intended purpose but was at the same time industry appropriate in that it supplied a level of entertainment value, we put our most ingenious thoughts forward — invented characters that made you smile but got the job done, set up well-considered and beguiling platforms from which to navigate — producing a couple of approaches that the customer was hard-pressed to choose between. Fanciful yes, frivolous no— there is a lot of substance, along with a stiff dose of wit, in each situation.

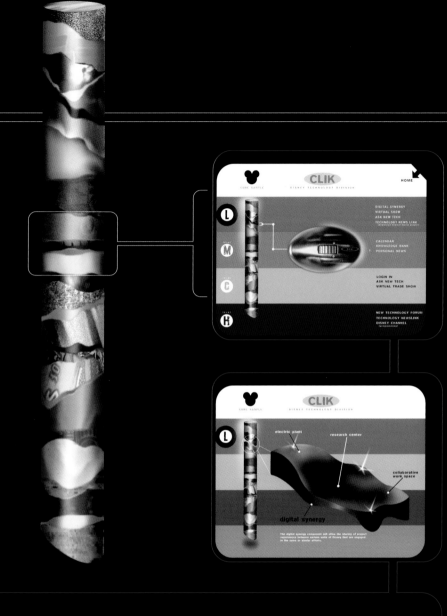

Do you remember where you were when Walt Disney died? You might have been seated in an arena of scientists, one of thirty that frantically removed Walt's head and prepared it for cryonic storage and certain reanimation in the future. Or — is this is the first you've heard about it?

The interface in this direction represents a core sample from Walt's frozen brain — four splash pages informing, convincing and defending the facts inside Walt's head. An Extract'o'Robotomator,® approximately 120 pixels wide and 80 pixels high, scans the core sample with its decoder arm. Click the red button and the Extract'o'Robotomator® pulls the core layer for closer scrutiny. The contents are then displayed in a window on the Extract'o'Robotomator.®

Because this is an intranet site and the information it contains is not available to the general public, there is no need to edit the private layers that Mr. Disney kept hidden deep within the frozen gray tundra of his mind. Once a core layer is pulled, let us say for Digital Synergy, mouseovers reveal the related groups in Disney and/or the contents for that specific topic. The Extract'o'Robotomator® is also a core layer search engine that can search the appropriate strata for the information you seek. Once it turned on us with its steel pixel scanning arm, pulled core layers of Jean's site, secured Kava Root Grafting Plans and posted them on the web. So, Steve had it put to sleep. We built a Nerf™ Extract'o'Robotomator® Model Duce the following year and it serves on our internal network even today.

APPLICATION
DISNEY INTRANET SITE   **1996**

CLIK!

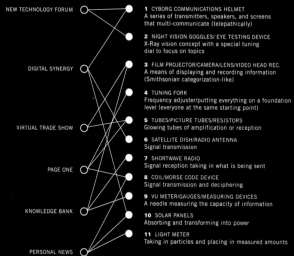

LEVEL ONE CATEGORIES   APPARATUS CHARACTERISTICS

NEW TECHNOLOGY FORUM

DIGITAL SYNERGY

VIRTUAL TRADE SHOW

PAGE ONE

KNOWLEDGE BANK

PERSONAL NEWS

1 CYBORG COMMUNICATIONS HELMET
A series of transmitters, speakers, and screens
that multi-communicate (telepathically)

2 NIGHT VISION GOGGLES/ EYE TESTING DEVICE
X-Ray vision concept with a special tuning
dial to focus on topics

3 FILM PROJECTOR/CAMERA/LENS/VIDEO HEAD REC.
A means of displaying and recording information
(Smithsonian categorization-like)

4 TUNING FORK
Frequency adjuster/putting everything on a foundation
level (everyone at the same starting point)

5 TUBES/PICTURE TUBES/RESISTORS
Glowing tubes of amplification or reception

6 SATELLITE DISH/RADIO ANTENNA
Signal transmission

7 SHORTWAVE RADIO
Signal reception taking in what is being sent

8 COIL/MORSE CODE DEVICE
Signal transmission and deciphering

9 VU METER/GAUGES/MEASURING DEVICES
A needle measuring the capacity of information

10 SOLAR PANELS
Absorbing and transforming into power

11 LIGHT METER
Taking in particles and placing in measured amounts

Deciphering Head Dresses [the chosen one]
Heads representing level one categories await their mission to inform Disney employees of leading technological trade secrets
shielded from the www. For example, Disney "Subject A" seeks information regarding digital animation for TV. Seems "Subject A"
has a Saturday morning 9am time slot for the Macintosh-based animated adventures of Grippy the neonatal Ape. "Subject A" needs
TV ratio rendering specifications. [Pan to screen/interface]. He mouses over the face entitled "Knowledge Bank" and checks the
pop-up menu for TV ratios. "There it is," he/she beams with excitement out loud, clicking the head that represents level one,
"Knowledge Bank." A face loads into the center portal and equips itself with a deciphering head dress that aids "Subject A" in the
search for "Ratios."

2.C

VIEWING DEVICE #2
PERSONALITY: C
TECHCENTER SITE: 1 - 7

2.A

PERSONALITY: A
TECHCENTER SITE: 2 - 1

The heads are very friendly. Each face has an inquisitive expression that reflects that of "Subject A" in his/her thirst for information. The client rejected adding cult slogans and bank account access forms (with us as the recipient). But other ideas for entering a password, then using code names in the registration splash screen, received approval from the top by a series of glacier clicks within Walt's head. They say, if you look him directly in the eye he will siphon 10% of your life force.

THOUGHT — Thought is deep inside himself. He has become sleepy. Very sleepy. And why not. This thought-bucket is doing the work of a small European city, searching for new ideas within the Disney intranet. The main fuselage is comprised of a distributor and ignition switches. The feasibility of the idea is measured in Joules on the gauge over his eye.

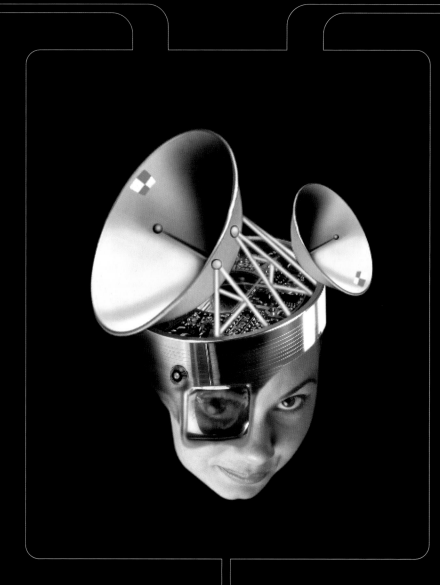

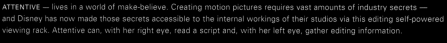

SMIRK — Smirk is sporting a Television/Video search head dress. The receptor dishes resemble a famous, nameless mouse personality. Unfortunately, portions of Smirk's head were removed in order to embed this stunning videotape head roller. If you need information about TV or video, whether for a current project or the newest techniques, this is the search cap for you.

ATTENTIVE — lives in a world of make-believe. Creating motion pictures requires vast amounts of industry secrets — and Disney has now made those secrets accessible to the internal workings of their studios via this editing self-powered viewing rack. Attentive can, with her right eye, read a script and, with her left eye, gather editing information.

...nder is made-up for the discovery of sounds. The search eyepiece is a volume ring through which he can meas...
...U — all sent via wavelength and heard on the fly with the built-in transmitter. If working with sound or music
...face like that, order me one, too.

...Puzzlement is in need of technical support for her computer. She has opted for the Cathode Ray tube
...bank of manuals. When a crash has got you puzzled, strap this 73 lb. monster to your block and learn
...change. The stunning nosepiece ensures hours of unfettered system garble.

CLIENT: Weyerhauser   PROJECT: paper promotion

PUBLICATION
COUGAR POSTER   1997

STANDSTROM
DESIGN 2

WEYERHAUSER — JOHN
CLEVELAND — LIEMER CROSS
DESIGN 1   DESIGN 3

TOLLESON
DESIGN 4

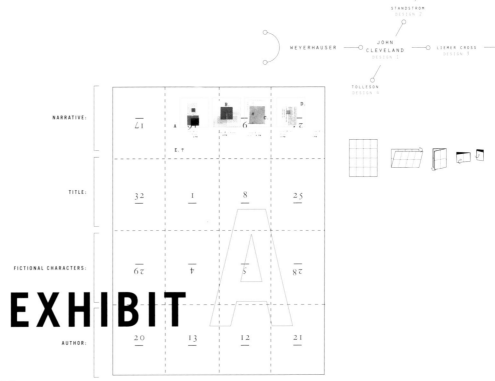

NARRATIVE:

TITLE:

FICTIONAL CHARACTERS:

EXHIBIT A

AUTHOR:

**IT'S AN
EPISODE**

11w   ) WE THINK YOU'LL LIKE IT

EXHIBIT B

**IT'S AN
ENDORSEMENT**   ) I LIKE IT

QUALIFICATION:

14h

KEY STATEMENTS:

EXHIBIT B1. - A 1997 2 PM	EXHIBIT B2. - A 1997 6 PM	EXHIBIT B3. - A 1997 9 PM	EXHIBIT B4. - A 1997 11 PM
0	**A-1**	**100%**	**98.7%**
COATING	**SMOOTHNESS**	**OPACITY**	**BRIGHTNESS**

FACTS:

A. B. C. D.

inwitness thereof:

SIGNATURE:

X _____

SAN FRANCISCO 1997

DESIGNED AND PRODUCED BY
TOLLESON DESIGN, sf/co
© 1997 TOLLESON DESIGN, sf/co

When approached by Weyerhauser Paper to contribute a poster to the campaign introducing a new product, our first inclination was to devise a piece that not only lent our name to the effort but interpreted the idea of endorsement in a fresh way. We designed the layout as if it were an unfolded signature, a large press sheet. On the "pages" laid out on the face of "Exhibit A," the story of "Pulp Killing," relating our belief in Weyerhauser's new, brighter, whiter product unfolds. In order to follow the tale, the reader has the option to view the piece as a poster or to fold the sheet down into a traditional book signature.

EXHIBIT

A

FRONT

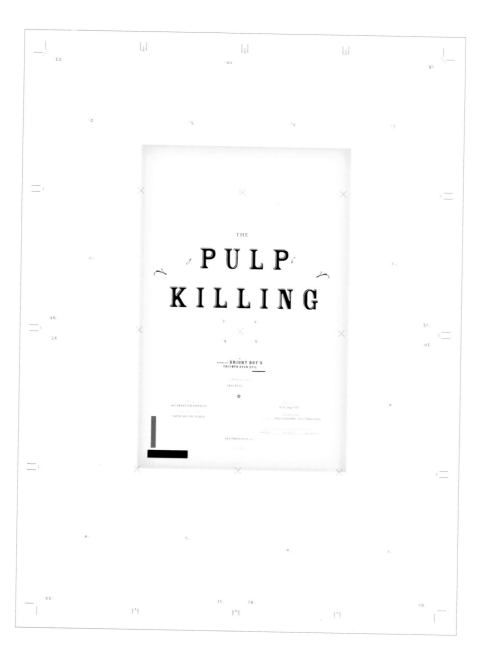

CLIENT: Weyerhauser   PROJECT: paper promotion

PUBLICATION
COUGAR POSTER

1997

When we presented the client with this option, they thought it was inventive and industry-appropriate — but was not what they were looking for. They had envisioned a more straightforward execution. It can be a challenge in situations such as this to find a way to attach your name to a product and render the endorsement in a manner that suits both the needs and taste of the client. So, we thought, if the desire is for a simple, direct communication from us, we will produce a fitting affidavit of our approval.

The resulting piece [Exhibit B] still contains some tongue-in-cheek elements. The front of the poster pits Cougar by Weyerhauser against the other "so-called" white papers. Cases are presented to compare brightness, coatings, smoothness and opacity and an authentically legal document details our belief in and commitment to this sheet – complete with notarized signatures.

EXHIBIT

A

BACK

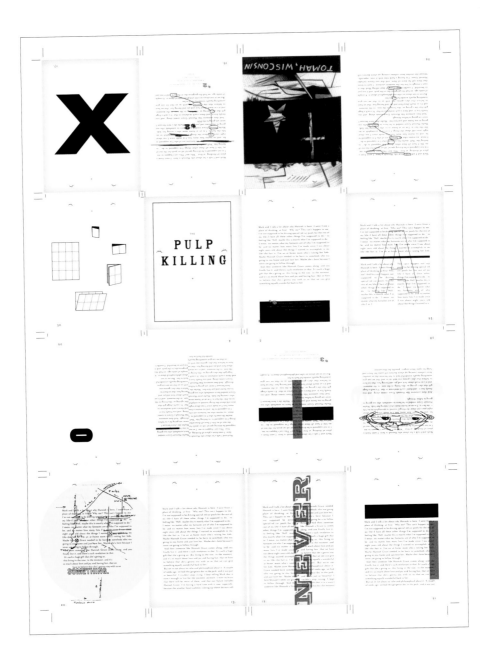

COUGAR by WEYERHAUSER

V.

SO-CALLED WHITE PAPER

EXHIBIT

B

FRONT

894.789H02

0 9-8

EXHIBIT A. –
8.1997
11: AM

150

SMOOTHNESS **A.**

COATING

NEVER!

EXHIBIT B. – 8.1997
2: PM

94%

C.

BRIGHTNESS

EXHIBIT C. –
8.1997 6: PM

OPACITY

97%

EXHIBIT D. –
8.1997
9: PM

SOLIDS 1. K

EXHIBITS

THE REAL STORY

AFFIDAVIT

| A-1 | 0 | 94% | 97% |

STORY OF **COUGAR OPAQUE**
AND THE TRIUMPH OVER AN EVIL OTHER

GREATNESS.

WEYERHAUSER PAPER CO.

ALAN LITHOGRAPH

PAPER-BUYING PUBLIC

COUGAR OPAQUE

X

TOLLESON DESIGN, sf/ca

TOLLESON DESIGN, sf/ca

PUBLICATION
1998 ASCEND ANNUAL REPORT

Our approach to the Ascend Communications 1998 Annual Report demonstrates Ascend's pioneering role in facilitating voice and data access. In recent years, the traffic over data communications lines has increased manyfold. Ascend's technolo allows voice and data to speak the same language while moving along existing telecommunications lines. This shared environment promotes a faster rate of transmis than was possible through traditional means.

CLIENT: Ascend Communications   PROJECT: annual report

It is costly to install new hardware solutions over a vast landscape; Ascend's solution makes existing hardware work harder and eliminates the need for costly retrofit. Illustrated by a series of scenic landscapes, the Ascend 1999 Annual Report conveys the company's ability to create new pathways and establish new directions, where none existed before. The photographic images in the annual reach into the distance, alluding to the way Ascend Communication is converging on a new technology.

DIR. Nº **7**.**0**

WHERE?

VOICE

D

C

FRAME RELAY

WIDE AREA NETWORK

REMOTE ACCESS

TIME

CLIENT: Ascend Communications   PROJECT: annual report

PUBLICATION
1999 ASCEND ANNUAL REPORT   1999

Overlaying the landscape images in the annual are a series of questions — and
answers. This dialog defines the Ascend business philosophy and marketing strategy.

ALCATEL
NEC
IBM
LUCENT TECHNOLOGIES

KEY PARTNERS

GTE INTER NET WORKING
PSINET
UUNET

FRONTIER   DIRECTTV
LEVEL 3   KINKO'S
WILLIAMS COMMUNICATIONS   NINTENDO OF AMERICA

                        ISPS   AT&T
ALTERNATIVE CARRIERS   ENTERPRISE   BELL ATLANTIC
                                          DEUTSCHE TELEKOM
                                          MCI WORLD.COM
                        CARRIERS   NTT

CUSTOMERS

WHO?

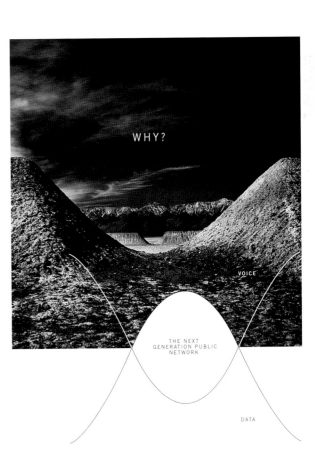

WHY?

VOICE

THE NEXT
GENERATION PUBLIC
NETWORK

MARKET
LEADERSHIP

DATA

Nº **41**

CLIENT: Ascend Communications   PROJECT: annual report

PUBLICATION
1999 ASCEND ANNUAL REPORT   1999

00 01

00

99

98

(ASND : AR-98 p 14-15

97

HOW IS ASCEND BUILDING THE NEXT-GENERATION PUBLIC NETWORK?

HOW?

00 01

00

99

98

97

☐ A. DATA TRAFFIC ON THE PUBLIC NETWORK IS GROWING EXPONENTIALLY. TO
ACCOMMODATE THIS GROWTH, SERVICE PROVIDERS ARE DIVERTING CAPITAL
EXPENDITURES AWAY FROM TRADITIONAL VOICE EQUIPMENT AND INTO NEXT-
GENERATION DATA NETWORKING EQUIPMENT.

☐ B. THE PSTN USES BANDWIDTH INEFFICIENTLY BY DEDICATING END-TO-END CIRCUITS
FOR EACH CALL.
FOR DATA TRAFFIC, THIS ARCHITECTURE IS EXTREMELY COSTLY. A NEW, INTEGRATED
NETWORK ARCHITECTURE IS NEEDED SO THAT BOTH VOICE AND DATA TRAFFIC CAN BE
HANDLED EFFICIENTLY AND COST EFFECTIVELY.

☐ C. THE TRADITIONAL PUBLIC SWITCHED TELEPHONE NETWORK (PSTN) IS NOT
DESIGNED TO HANDLE LARGE AMOUNTS OF DATA TRAFFIC. AS DATA TRAFFIC CONTINUES
TO INCREASE, IT DRIVES THE NEED FOR SERVICE PROVIDERS TO BUILD A NEW PUBLIC
NETWORK ARCHITECTURE.

☑ D. ALL OF THE ABOVE

96

95

95

94

CLIENT: Nike   PROJECT: environmentalretail

POINT OF SALE, RETAIL
NIKE TUNED AIR BASKETBALL SHOES   1999

CONCEPTS APPLICABLE TO TARGET MARKET

CONCEPT #1 *TUNE IN*
A visual palette derived from the name itself (Tuned Air). Other elements include radio and television aesthetics.

CONCEPT #2 *LIGHTER THAN AIR*
Conveying the victory over gravity as athletes float effortlessly above obstacles.

CONCEPT #3 *AVERAGE*
Displaying the average end-user, possibly at his home — as if to take the awe out of and reveal the essence that anyone can participate.

CONCEPT #4 *URBAN / SUBURBAN*
Displaying the many facets of individuals who play the game. From Iowa Elementary School Yard games to New York City street ball. By extruding someone from his or her element and placing them outside that element, diversity is displayed. And a camaraderie is established by the fact that wherever you're from, just shoot the ball.

Tn
AIR
TUNEDAIR

4

2

3

1

CONCEPT

BASKETBALL SHOES

nike

Force

Flight

Uptempo

Champs

Kid's FootLocl

VENATAR GROUP

FootLo

Lad

VISUAL PALETTE OF JUXTAPOSITION

The game provides a full-spectrum perspective from the smallest hometown to the most highly populated environment. Crossing boundaries in style and aesthetics but remaining purely and simple defined.

s / 1   s / 1   s / 1

D   E   F

s / 2

F

s / 3

su / 4

F

su / 5

A

u / 5

A

u / 5

A

SUBURBAN

URBAN

POINT OF SALE; RETAIL
NIKE TUNED AIR BASKETBALL SHOES   1999

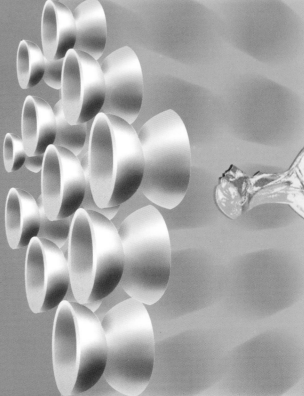

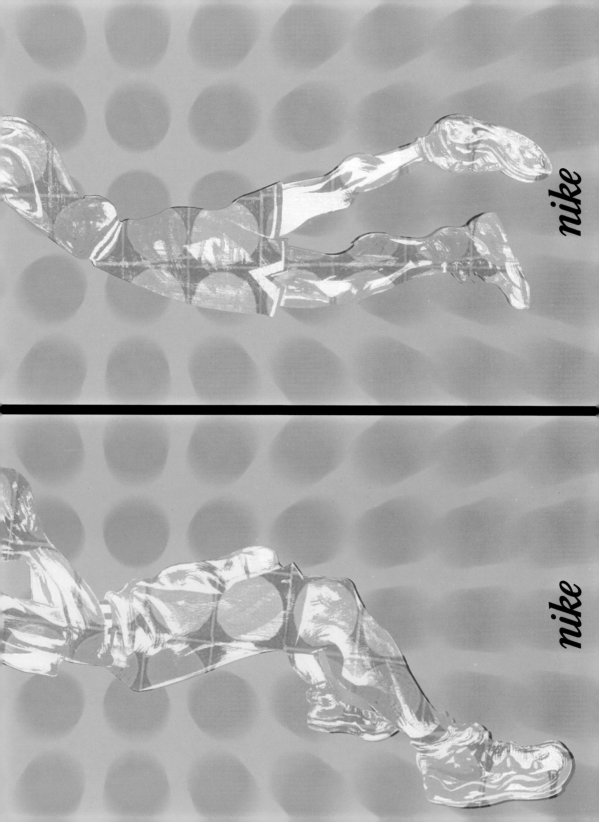

To achieve increased yield and reduce time-to-market, Asyst Technologies provides complete wafer isolation technology, inventory management and automation systems for the semiconductor and related industries. Specializing in the delivery of cleanroom air and gases and facilitating fab retrofit through robotic technologies, the Asyst success rate can literally be measured in particles per square inch.

For a company whose goal is to produce environments so clean they approach a vacuum state in terms of purity, the Asyst metaphor revealed itself in cold, austere, sharply defined terms. The difficulty of describing an abstract process lies in finding a visual equivalent for something invisible/unseen. As we constructed the Asyst materials, the cleanroom influenced everything we did. We found ways in print and manufacturing to give form to a substantially insubstantial set of achievements. Since the sale is made at the senior level, Asyst's services had to be marketed to a sophisticated, no-nonsense audience in an immediate and compelling manner.

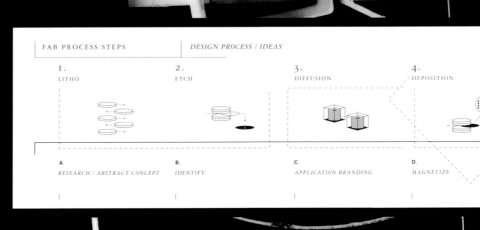

FAB PROCESS STEPS		DESIGN PROCESS / IDEAS	
1. LITHO	2. ETCH	3. DIFFUSION	4. DEPOSITION
A. RESEARCH / ABSTRACT CONCEPT	B. IDENTIFY	C. APPLICATION BRANDING	D. MAGNETIZE

FREMONT, CA 945...
510.661.5225   FAX: 510.661.5110
PAGER: 800.923.7407
INTERNET: whansen@asyst.com

ΛSYST

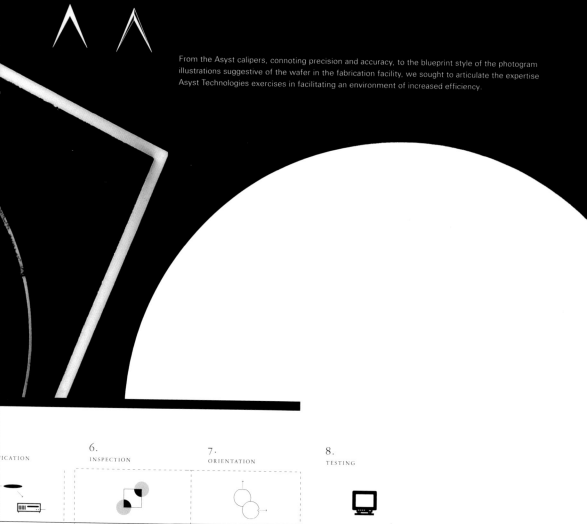

From the Asyst calipers, connoting precision and accuracy, to the blueprint style of the photogram illustrations suggestive of the wafer in the fabrication facility, we sought to articulate the expertise Asyst Technologies exercises in facilitating an environment of increased efficiency.

FICATION

6.
INSPECTION

7.
ORIENTATION

8.
TESTING

IZE

F.
EXAMINE

G.
EXAMINE

H.
PUBLISH

CLIENT: Asyst Technologies   PROJECT: id / ar / collateral / event

PUBLICATION
ASYST TECHNOLOGIES 1994 ANNUAL REPORT   1995

I X I0⁻⁵

I X I0⁻⁵

I X I0⁻⁵

I X I0⁻⁵

I X I0⁻⁵

I X I0⁻⁵

I X I0⁻⁵

I X I0⁻⁵

I X I0⁻⁵

I X I0⁻⁵

AVERAGE NUMBER OF PARTICLES

CLASS 10

CLASS 1

$$(>0.1\mu) \, / \, ft^3$$

MATERIAL
REFERENCE

A.   CLEAN WHITE

B.   DIE HOLE

C.   ENGRAVING PROCESS

D.   METALLIC INK / GROMMET

E.   CONCEPTUAL
      ILLUSTRATION

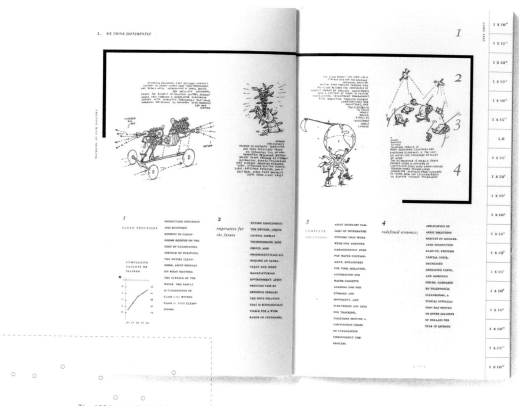

The 1994 annual report for Asyst Technologies employed multiple graphic techniques to evoke the atmosphere of the fabrication process. The raised character of the engraved printing and illustration simulating the feel of silicon on the wafer surface, the laser-cut hole that drills through the pages of the book suggesting the singular particle and, not least, the theme itself — "it's not what you think" — all asked the reader to look again at this company's capabilities.

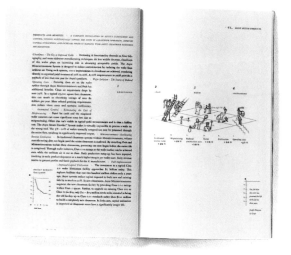

PUBLICATION
ASYST LAB BOOK AND INVITATION   1995

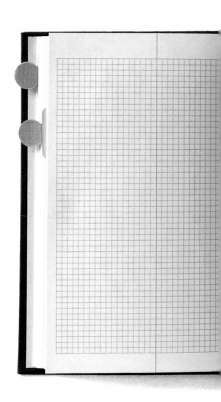

MATERIAL
REFERENCE

A. SIZE

B. CONTENT / ORGANIZATION

C. METAL

D. ETCH PROCESS

E. METALLIC INK

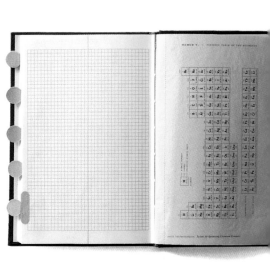

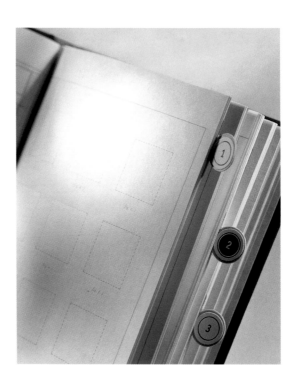

Environmental influences inspired this series of trade show promotions created for Asyst in 1995. These "smart" pieces beg the viewer to find the connection to the Asyst line of business. Among the technological influences in the products we created were the etched metal Rolodex card, sent as an invitation to a demonstration; a lab book give-away to hold notes and concepts for your newest enterprise.

PUBLICATION
ASYST SEMICON MATERIALS   1996

A.

MATERIAL
REFERENCE

A.   MAGNETIC COVERS

B.   PROCESS VISUALIZATION

C.   LABORATORY PROCESS

D.   EXAMINATION
      ILLUSTRATION

In 1996, a series of announcements on round wafer-like coasters that arrived in a sterile medical tin; an accordion-fold announcement sandwiched between covers held in place magnetically; a poster folded into the format of a road map announcing expanded capabilities and Asyst's propulsion along the route to a new round of successes.

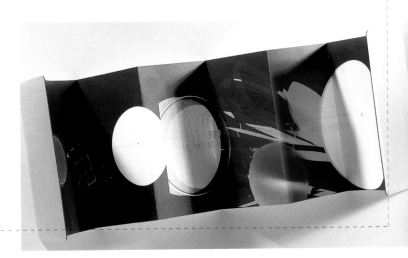

B.

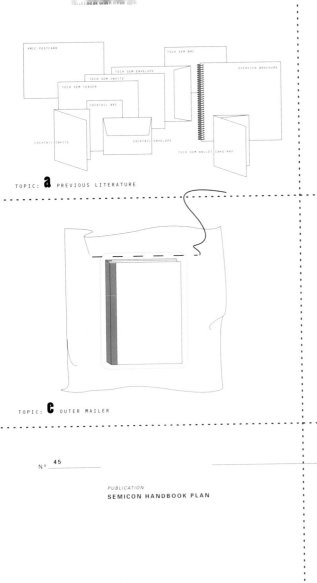

TOPIC: **a** PREVIOUS LITERATURE

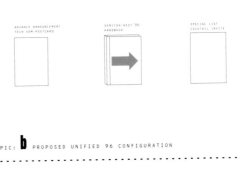

ADVANCE ANNOUNCEMENT
TECH SEM-POSTCARD   SEMICON/WEST 96-
HANDBOOK   SPECIAL LIST
COCKTAIL INVITE

TOPIC: **b** PROPOSED UNIFIED 96 CONFIGURATION

TOPIC: **e** OUTER MAILER

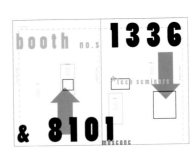

booth no.s **1336**
tech seminars
& 8101 moscone

TOPIC: **f** CITY / MOSCONE / BOOTH MAPS

N° **45**

PUBLICATION
SEMICON HANDBOOK PLAN

CLIENT: Applied Materials   PROJECT: conference materials

1996

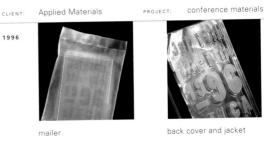

mailer   back cover and jacket

TOPIC: **i** COVERS

july 16 -   enabling technology

TOPIC: **k** SEMINAR SCHEDULES

contacts   contacts

TOPIC: **l** EXHIBITION NOTE SECTION

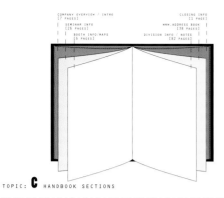

TOPIC: **c** HANDBOOK SECTIONS

APPLIED OVERVIEW
-TITLE PAGE
-SEMICON WELCOME / INVITATION
-INTRODUCTION / CO. OVERVIEW
-MISSION STATEMENT

SEMINAR INFORMATION
-TECHNICAL SEMINAR SERIES
  -TOPICS
  -SPEAKERS
  -SCHEDULE
-THREE DAY PLANNER/DATE BOOK
-OTHER EVENT INFO

BOOTH INFORMATION
-MAPS
  -SAN FRANCISCO
  -MOSCONE-HALL, BOOTH AND
   TECHNOLOGY SEM LOCATOR

DIVISION / PROCESS INFORMATION PAGES
-ETCH
-CVD
-PVD
-TPT
-IBSS
-300MM
-PSI
-MICROCONTAMINATION

WWW.TOPIC NOTE-BOOK PAGES
-SEARCH ENGINE TOPICS:

CONTACT PAGES
-DATEBOOK / PREREGISTRATION

GUIDEBOOK PAGES
-RESTAURANT, TAXIS, ETC.

SEPARATE MAP
-DETAILED BOOTH DIAGRAMS WITH
 PRODUCT LOCATIONS

TOPIC: **d** SECTION CONTENT

TOPIC: **g** TRAINING/PROFESSIONAL GROUP

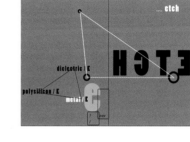

TOPIC: **h** PROCESS OVERVIEW

1.**0** / 10.**0**

TOPIC: **m** HANDBOOK SECTIONS

When Applied Materials asked us to participate in the madness of trade show design, we asked them to consider that, perhaps, there was a better way. We took nine separate communications — everything from a booth map, seminar times, divisional information, product literature, local restaurant, taxi and hotel data, and a place to enter notes — and synthesized them into one small volume so that the attendees had fewer separate items to carry around with them.

TOPIC: **j**

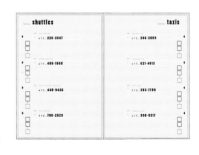

TOPIC: **n** CITY GUIDE YELLOW PAGES

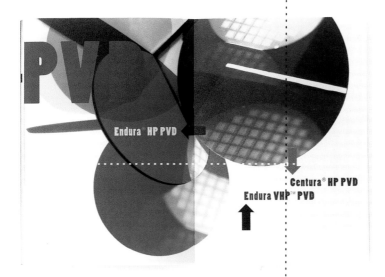

Endura® HP PVD

Centura® HP PVD

Endura VHP™ PVD

shift

CLIENT: Applied Materials   PROJECT: conference materials

PUBLICATION
SEMICON HANDBOOK

1996

The consolidated information took the form of a small handbook, just the size to fit into a pocket or pocketbook, that was covered in a metal jacket, a material that is used in the Applied Materials manufacturing facilities.

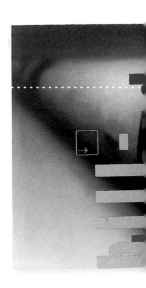

Visit our worldwide web site @

http://www.Applied Materials.com

WWW.

return

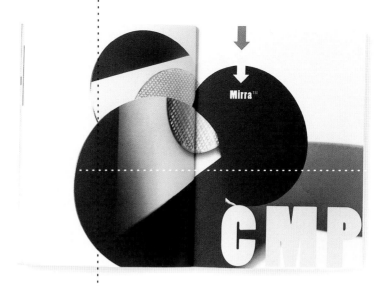

Mirra™

CMP

→

DIR. N°   **2**·**0**

enter

return

The whole thing was mailed inside a sealed plastic pouch
evoking the sterile conditions of a lab. The volume had
enough useful information in it so that it could be saved as
a reference piece after the show.

billboard

Highway 101 North
and Grand Avenue

info

news
events

1 - analyst breakfast : july

2 - press event : july 17

NVidia designs, develops, markets and sells highly integrated 3D multimedia accelerator chips for the mainstream PC market. They are innovators in the development of this high-speed enabling technology. In 1994, when NVidia was a start-up venture with few strategic alliances, they asked us to help them develop not only their visual identity but to devise a means to exhibit the capabilities of their product. In order to demonstrate the technology that would become responsible for "driving multimedia to the limit of human perception" we had to concoct environments that would show off their ingenuity.

While the future of the technology would later see broad-based application in the CAD environment, in education and in many yet-to-be-conceived situations, at the time of our initial encounter the only platform that offered both audio and visual expression for the powers of the NV chip was the 3D gaming setting. The ability to render at "twitch speed" and enable concurrent media streaming was being delivered only in the arcade graphics setting where performance is everything. So, with a very limited set of supporting evidence, we established an environment for the marketing of NVidia as possessing the power to "transform the PC into the ultimate multimedia machine."

1.0

DIR. N°

id / marketing collateral

PROJECT·

NVidia

CLIENT·

TO HAVE INTERACTIVE MULTIMEDIA
YOU MUST HAVE
THE INTEGRATION OF
THESE 4 COMPONENTS

1. DIRECT SOUND
2. DIRECTDRAW/3D-DDI/REALITY LABS
3. DIRECT INPUT
4. SURROUND VIDEO

nV

nV

SGW·88KGAH01
H220M9405
MALTA

nV₁

SGW·88KGAH01
H220M9405
MALTA

1
GRAPHIC

WINDOWS 95

No. 1

N. . . . . .

. . . *95*

WINDOWS 95 - - - - - 3 AUDIO

2 VIDEO

4 DIGITAL INPUT

NV1 WINDOWS 95 MULTIMEDIA ACCELERATOR

THE ENGINE   NVIDIA'S DELIVERY OF THAT VISION

1.
2.
3.
4.

DIRECT SOUND
CONCURRENT
HIGH-FIDELITY
AUDIO ENGINE
DIRECT DRAW/3D-DDI/REALITY LABS
REAL-TIME PHOTOREALISTIC
3D GRAPHICS
2D GRAPHICS ACCELERATOR
DIRECT INPUT
DIRECT INPUT
DIGITAL JOYSTICK PORT
SURROUND VIDEO
VIDEO ACCELERATION
VIDEO TEXTURING
SPECIAL EFFECTS

1994

NVIDIA PRESS KIT

We designed the press box as a souvenir to serve as a reminder of this forward-thinking new company long after the event. A screaming red-orange container which housed a suite of marketing briefs was inserted into a heavy gauge metal portfolio. The substantial package closed with a spring tension wire. In an industry where so many players are competing for a limited amount of attention, the NVidia materials were bent on grabbing market share. The impact of this limited edition kit was certainly more visual than conceptual but it had the desired effect — and was twice reissued.

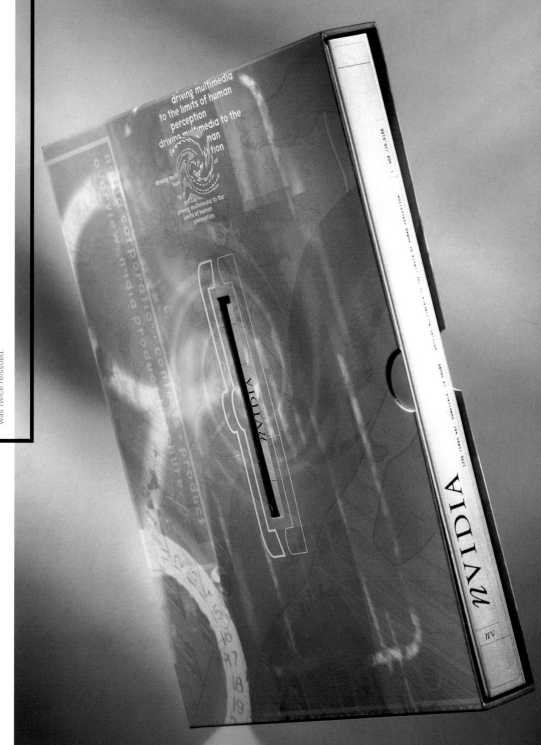

PUBLICATION
NVIDIA PACKAGING

CLIENT: NVidia

1995

PROJECT: id / marketing collateral

DIR. N° **2.0**

The interim product packaging for NVidia's first chip was a black construction, striking a sharp note of contrast to the other attention-grabbing, color-saturated communications promoting the group.

For a trade event in the subsequent year, we worked with NVidia to devise some fresh imagery for a collection of posters that would decorate their booth. Along with these we developed a giveaway that took the form of an internet address book.

1996

PUBLICATION
NVIDIA EVENT POSTER

CLIENT: Virgin Interactive   PROJECT: game catalog

PUBLICATION
VIRGIN ADRENALINE EXPERIMENT   1997

The diagram to the right is representative of the elaborate intertwining of tasks that comprised the E3 Catalog for Virgin Interactive. The effect of the chart is one of a visual timecard that depicts the overlapping of roles and the interweaving of processes as the booklet took shape. Simultaneous with developing the storyline and characters,

we generated copy and photographed the subjects of the experiments, their images altered electronically and collaged into the gaming landscapes. We designed pages with high-resolution graphics in place (to save re-creating the files in mechanical form later on — since there was to be no "later on" — and the text was edited in-position.

TASK LEGEND ————

■ CONCEPT DEVELOPMENT
▮ STORYLINE NARRATION
▮ CHARACTER CREATION
▮ IMAGE GENERATION
▯ CHARACTER / ENVIRONMENT
  ASSEMBLY

ONE DAY

ALL OF THIS HAPPENED IN A BOX WITH NO HUMAN CONTACT FROM THE VIRGIN INTERACTIVE PEOPLE. WE RECEIVED THE ASSIGNMENT THROUGH E-MAILS WITH A SERIES OF ATTACHED FILES. THE STORY, ITS ENVIRONMENTS AND CHARACTERS DEVELOPED ENTIRELY INSIDE THE COMPUTER. WE SUPPLIED PDF SKETCHES TO THE CLIENT OVER THE INTERNET THROUGH A SECURED FTP SITE. IN THIS WAY, THE STORYLINE DEVELOPED LIKE A GAME — IT WAS AN ADVENTURE IN ROLE-PLAYING THAT EVOLVED AS THE PROJECT MOVED AHEAD AT LIGHTNING PACE.

When assigned the project of producing the Virgin Interactive catalog of coming attractions for the E3 event in 1997, we found ourselves with very little resources and time. The only materials available to us for this short turnaround project were a copy brief on the games for the coming season and a handful of low-res screen shots. Anything else that we were to include had to be the product of our imagination.

As we brainstormed possible scenarios, we asked ourselves a series of questions about why people play games — specifically high-speed, realistic electronic games. Our answers led us in the direction of our ultimate solution. Games provide an adrenaline rush, the thrill of functioning at "twitch speed." From that platform, we created a fictional electronic environment in which a renegade scientist administered a series of adrenaline experiments to a group of subjects, and cataloged the results along with the Virgin offerings.

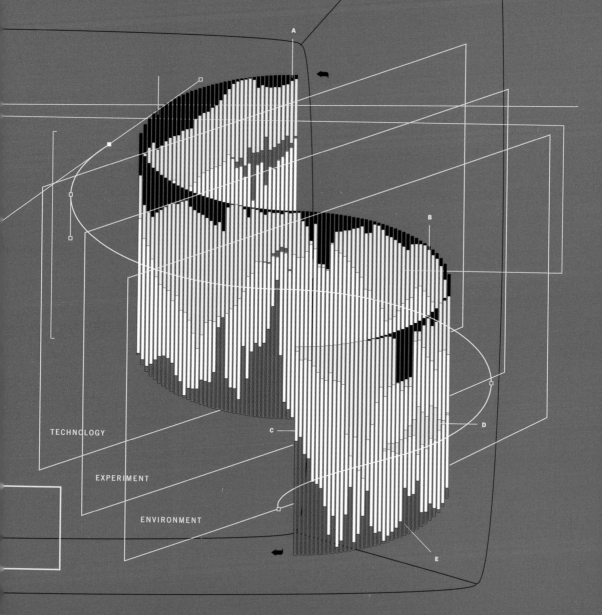

TECHNOLOGY

EXPERIMENT

ENVIRONMENT

PUBLICATION
VIRGIN ADRENALINE EXPERIMENT   1997

The story of the evil Dr. Jolt, from the Virgin Interactive Department of Research and Development and his group of willing (?) subjects is superimposed upon the latest offerings from Virgin's interactive gaming library. The narrative about this "other world" creates an environment for the listing of products and gives it an appeal to which this edgy, hip audience can relate.

that piece took 14 hours

C 2: **B, 1.1, 12**   C 3: **I, 3.3, 2**

Acting entirely on their own, a top-level R&D team hired Dr. Mobius Jolt to conduct a series of experiments measuring and analyzing the volatile relationship between adrenaline and Virgin Interactive games — using live test subjects. It was known that this team had been working with the most talented developers in the field on a handful of classified projects. As the following report details, all of these were games capable of inducing dangerously high levels of adrenaline production. In addition, Virgin's forays into the boundless capabilities of Internet-based entertainment have resulted in the creation of several post-millennial games that are currently too extreme for the contemporary human mind. Apparently, these were unleashed on the test subjects as well. It should be noted that none of Dr. Jolt's credential, personal history, psychological profile, etc. were given even the most basic scrutiny, and that his adrenaline testing was not officially authorized. We also wish to stress that no living things were injured during the testing phase, and that the valuable information yielded by the study will stand as industry benchmarks for years to come. However, due to Dr. Jolt's somewhat unorthodox techniques, we cannot overemphasize enough that this report is not for the squeamish or faint-hearted.

CATALOG CONCEPT:

ADRENALINE TESTING — PRELIMINARY RESEARCH REVEALED THAT VIRGIN INTERACTIVE GAMES CAN AFFECT NOT JUST PLAYERS, BUT SPECTATORS AS WELL. TO DEFEND MYSELF AGAINST ANY SORT OF INCREASED ADRENALINE PRODUCTION, I UNDERWENT A PROCEDURE THAT REPLACED MY EYEBALLS WITH NIPPLES. (INTERESTING — MY SUBJECTS WILL FEED ON THE KNOWLEDGE I GATHER, BUT I CANNOT SEE). WHILE I CANNOT ABSOLUTELY GUARANTEE THE SAFETY OF EACH SUBJECT, I WILL DO MY BEST TO ENSURE THAT THEIR EXPERIENCE WITH VIRGIN INTERACTIVE GAMES IS METICULOUSLY DOCUMENTED FOR POSTERITY — AND, OF COURSE, TO GARNER A CERTAIN AMOUNT OF WELL-DESERVED RECOGNITION FOR MY PART IN THIS MOMENTOUS EXPERIMENT.

PUBLICATION
VIRGIN ADRENALINE EXPERIMENT   1997

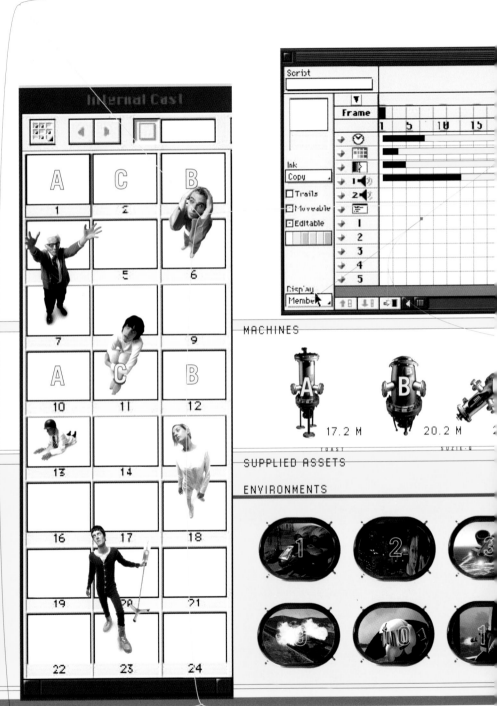

CHAPTER 1: **A, 2.2, 10**

CATALOG **SCORE CODE:**   C 3: **D, 1.1**

We assembled characters and plotted elements and experimental apparatus into a palette that was reorganized for each new scenario. The wildly disparate settings and allegories established by the games are populated by Dr. Jolt's victims. Players, backdrops and instruments are composed into dramatic sequences which are strung together through the travels of the subjects, as they jump from game to game, looking for the next "rush."

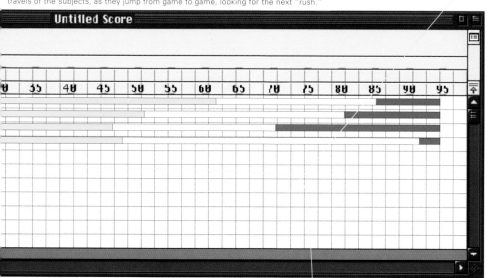

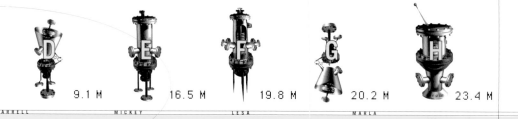

9.1 M   16.5 M   19.8 M   20.2 M   23.4 M

DARRELL   MICKEY   LESA   MARLA

G, 4.1, 7 ᶜ³: D, 1.1, 4 ᶜ³: F, 1.2, 6 ᶜ³: H, 2.1, 7 ᶜ³: D, 2.1, 5 ᶜ³: I, 3.3, 2
D, 1.1, 4 ᶜ²: G, 4.1, 7 ᶜ²: E, 4.2, 9 ᶜ²: B, 1.1, 12 ᶜ²: A, 2.2, 16 ᶜ²: F, 3.1,

DIR N° **3.2**

game catalog

PROJECT

Virgin Interactive

CLIENT 1997

PUBLICATION
VIRGIN ADRENALINE EXPERIMENT

N° **47**

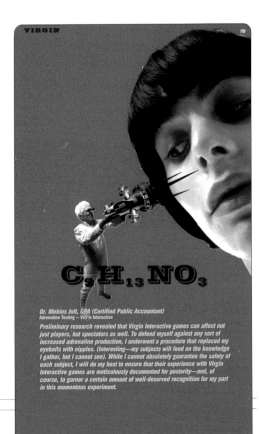

$$C_9H_{13}NO_3$$

Dr. Mobius Jolt, CPA (Certified Public Accountant)
Adrenaline Testing -- Virgin Interactive

Preliminary research revealed that Virgin Interactive games can affect not just players, but spectators as well. To defend myself against any sort of increased adrenaline production, I underwent a procedure that replaced my eyeballs with nipples. (Interesting—my subjects will feed on the knowledge I gather, but I cannot see). While I cannot absolutely guarantee the safety of each subject, I will do my best to ensure that their experience with Virgin Interactive games are meticulously documented for posterity—and, of course, to garner a certain amount of well-deserved recognition for my part in this momentous experiment.

SABRE ACE: CONFLICT OVER KOREA

RALLY CHAMPIONSHIP
INTERNATIONAL OFF-ROAD RACING
PC CD-ROM

DESCRIPTION

Rally Championship: Facing the world's toughest test on wheels —the Network Q RAC Rally, drivers experience true rally car physics and performance over 28 grueling stages. Officially endorsed by the RAC Motorsport Division, the only way you'll beat it is to jump in a car and do the real thing.

PLATFORM: PC CD-ROM   **WEB:** www.vie.com

FEATURES:
* CHOOSE FROM SIX FULLY LICENSED, FULL SPEC, RALLY-BRED CARS
* DAY/NIGHT MODES WITH MULTIPLE ROAD AND WEATHER CONDITIONS
* MULTIPLAYER OPTION: 8-DRIVER NETWORK PLAY
* FOUR PLAY MODES: ARCADE, INDIVIDUAL, TIME TRIAL AND CHAMPIONSHIP

DOCTOR'S LOG:
Entry #81 (Subject #001-m): Sent my preliminary findings to Virgin R&D this week, they are quite pleased, as am I. Virgin is also extremely curious about #001-m, who today spoke his first words in several days. Many questions about subject's emotional state. I have confirmed that the constant smile on #001-m's face is directly linked to the high adrenaline levels, but in order to minimize speculation, I have requisitioned a new excitement probing device, the ManiaManager 2.0, to use while subject plays Rally Championship. This tool measures adrenaline levels and displays vivid pictures of the subject's internal response to excitement. As #001-m races across countrysides, snow and mountains, I'll just sit back and watch his heart race.

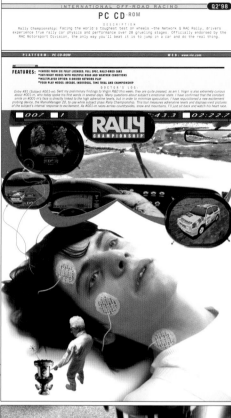

NHL POWERPLAY™ '98
HOCKEY
SONY-PLAYSTATION / WINDOWS® 95 CD-ROM

DOCTOR'S LOG:
Entry #109 (Subject #001-m): #001-m is not well. His exposure to the battery of Virgin products, along with the accompanying overdoses of adrenaline, has left him terribly weakened. In spite of his condition, he is in wonderfully high spirits, which carried him a long way in NHL Powerplay '98. He upgraded his dental plan and delivered some head-clearing checks in the process. Nevertheless, the 3-D environment proved to be too much for him in his weakened state. If only I had fed him. My enthusiasm for this study has become so great that I've completely overlooked his need for traditional nourishment. Lying on the ice, #001-m looked me straight in the nipples and told me he loved me like a father. I can't help but feel partially responsible for his deterioration. Those 3-D players are bigger, faster, and well-fed.

PLATFORM: Sony PlayStation / Windows®95   **WEB:** www.vie.com

heist
ORGANIZED CRIME GAME   Q1'98
WINDOWS® 95 CD-ROM

DESCRIPTION

Heist taps into society's fascination with crime and the ceaseless battle of wits between villains and police by allowing gamers to break the law. Players run and administer a professional burglary crew through more than 20 high-stake missions. Recruiting specialists, laying down bribes, outsmarting sophisticated security systems and finally, escaping from the authorities are just some of the risks players take to amass a huge fortune for the final goal—an early and easy retirement.

PLATFORM: Windows® 95 CD-ROM   **WEB:** www.vie.com

NOTE: TOP SECRET PROJECT CODED TRANSMISSION

Entry #124 (Subject #002-f): #001-m remains in a stupor while hands and feet whirl in the air as if he's riding an invisible unicycle and of course useless to me. Earlier #001-m mentioned a girl (#002-f), whose craving for interactive gaming has placed in a twelve step program in Paris. The French Council was happy to relinquish the burden, and I filled out 48 forms for her release, which stated her current condition. Oddly enough she was already versed in Heist and her hide-out was bloated with paintings from the Louvre. I lured the highly refined #002-f with Russian Caviar into a crime ring where I could monitor her adrenaline levels. This job would take time and I. Where's the watch? Where's my wallet? Where's my Adren3 metronome?

HEIST

NHL POWERPLAY™ '98
HOCKEY
SONY-PLAYSTATION / WINDOWS® 95 CD-ROM

DESCRIPTION

NHL Powerplay '98. Step into the skates of the NHL's greatest talents—skating, checking and hooking your way down the ice toward the goal. Once in scoring position, you can even track season stats, or create and trade players in NHL Powerplay '98. Go head-to-head with goalies who mimic their real-life counterparts to ward off every attempted shot. All of this realistic action is captured in an on-the-fly 3-D environment for both Windows 95 and PlayStation.

PLATFORM: Sony PlayStation / Windows®95   **WEB:** www.vie.com

* THE MOST AUTHENTIC HOCKEY MOVES AND ADVANCED AI FOR TRULY REALISTIC NHL ACTION
* EXPANDED COACH TEAM FEATURE TO CONTROL TEAM STRATEGY
* ABILITY TO TRACK STATS OVER AN ENTIRE SEASON, TRADE AND EVEN CREATE PLAYERS
* THE MOST IN-YOUR-FACE IMMERSIVE HOCKEY GRAPHICS-3-D ENVIRONMENT AND MOTION-CAPTURED PLAYER MODELS

DOCTOR'S LOG:
Entry #114 (Subject #001-m): With the absence of my eyeballs, I have developed a sort of telepathic second sight. I can see #001-m's fear: he is running on pure adrenaline, and is headed for a complete breakdown. He was traded to Ecuador and set in the wing position. Learning to play left-handed so that his right hand removed the fee for signing 8X10 glossies, #001-m's stats rose to the top of the league. I managed to swing a deal with Mongolia in order to get #001-m traded to an expansion team, but the adrenaline level thrust him into extended play. 001-m was like a son, and his contributions were invaluable, but if his body is found, my research might be seriously curtailed. It's not that I don't care but I still have test subject #002-f. She's new and fresh.

NHL POWERPLAY™ '98

Entry #47 (Subject #001-m): Abnormally high adrenaline production: attempts to counter it with soothing music and warm milk have proved futile. #001-m uses uncontrollable speed to feed his adrenaline habit. Eyeballs have inverted and become windows into his own thoughts; looking him in the eyes is like looking through a car's windshield at the driver within. Subject displays a complete lack of touch with reality — Virgin's HellRacer has become his world. Each target obliterated, opponent defeated, and race won adds fuel to his already maniacal excitement. Subject keeps spending oversized winner's checks on power and speed accessories to, quote, "Deck out my ride."

SUBSPACE

THE INTERNET GAME

INTERNET WWW

PLATFORM: Internet **WEB:** www.vie.com

DOCTOR'S LOG:

Entry #151 (Subject #002-f): Responding like a fish to water, #002-f has mastered space flight in record time. Each increased level of adrenaline affects her like a growth pill; her reflexes and motor controls have all shown marked increases in speed and agility as she careens through space vying for power-ups to improve her ship. Using SubSpace's on-screen chat system, she is developing a reputation for her razor-sharp wit, throwing out good-natured taunts to the opponents she destroys. Subject insists that it's all just good clean fun, so do her countless cult followers who cover their eyes when she speaks and call out "J'Arc?, A guy in France made a face at us. Will you have them obliterated?"

THE INTERNET GAME

INTERNET WWW

Q3'97

DESCRIPTION

SubSpace is an Internet-only real-time action game that is massively multi-player, allowing pilots to fly against hundreds of other players in an enormous space battle with people from around the world in team or individual play, by skill level. Players jockey through space collecting power-ups that will increase their ship's firepower, armament, maneuverability, and special weapons. Jump into the Chaos Zone, team up and win the flag game, or just score big and compete against the world's best in the Expert Zone.

QUOTE: "PC Games (A) List...Simple to start, easy to play well and thoroughly engrossing...Asteroids for the online generation." PC Games

FEATURES:
• ENGAGE IN REAL-TIME BATTLE AGAINST HUNDREDS OF HUMAN PLAYERS
• COMPETE AGAINST THE BEST PILOTS IN THE WORLD IN THE EXPERT ZONE
• PLOT STRATEGIES, BUILD ATTACK PLANS AND TAUNT IN REAL-TIME
• CONSTANTLY EVOLVING GAME WITH MORE THAN 100,000 PLAYERS AND 150 REVISIONS

DOCTOR'S LOG:

Entry #207 (Subject #002-f): Acute inability to resolve disputes through peaceful means. Subject has assembled a squadron of top-notch interstellar pilots; under her masterful command, they wreak havoc and fear throughout the www, trouncing all of their opponents, collecting enormous scores, and spewing snide remarks. #002-f has become as overbearing and arrogant as a Roman emperor. She can now control the game internally. I've lost contact with #002-f and believe her to be entirely catatonic on the surface. Yesterday's catharsis exposed her unstoppable drive to control the www. She eats without thinking. She moves in the shadows. She wants to hurt me.

SUBSPACE

VIRGIN CONCLUSIONS

PRECISION ADRENALINE RESEARCH AND DEVELOPMENT RESULTS

RESULTS

P3—Sabre Ace produced high adrenaline levels, manual dexterity, and delusions of grandeur.

P4—HellRacer produced high adrenaline levels, lightning reflexes, and a voracious appetite for speed.

P5—Broken Sword: The Smoking Mirror produced high adrenaline levels and problem-solving ability from situations of extreme bewilderment.

P6—Rally Championship produced high adrenaline levels, incredible adaptability, and a fairly serious speed fixation.

P7—Heist produced high adrenaline levels, nerves of steel, well-developed night vision, and extremely high manual dexterity.

P8-9—NHL Powerplay™ '98 produced high adrenaline levels, a fantastic slap shot, and a few loose teeth.

P10-11—SubSpace produced high adrenaline levels, unusually broad peripheral vision, ruthless, arrogant behavior and a wisecracking mouth.

$C_9H_{13}NO_3$

CONCLUSIONS:

Virgin Interactive games proved to induce extremely high levels of adrenaline in the male and female human test subjects used in this study, a very satisfying outcome. There were, of course, certain other side effects noted above that were not quite so pleasing.

— Mobius Jolt, C.P.A.

Virgin Interactive ended 1996 with sales of over $250 million, and nine offices worldwide. Offices that employ over 600 people producing award-winning products, marketing and an ever-expanding affiliate label distribution program. The summer of 1997 has already seen the announcement of key partnerships with Paramount, Disney and Capcom resulting in products such as Star Trek Voyager, Hercules for PlayStation and Resident Evil for PC. Virgin is always on the lookout for new development talent and publishers seeking distribution.

throwing out good-natured taunts to the opponents she destroys. Subject insists that it's all just good clean fun, and so do her countless cult followers who cover their eyes when she speaks and calls out "J'Arc"?, a guy in France made a face at us. Will you have them obliterated?"

Entry #151 (subject #002-f): Responding like a fish to water, #002-f has mastered space flight in record time. Each increased level of adrenaline affects her like a growth pill; her reflexes and motor controls have all shown marked increase in speed and agility as she careens through space vying for power-ups to improve her ship. Using Sub-Space's on-screen chat system, she is developing a reputation for her razor-sharp wit,

4.54

td responsibilities

Designer –
Try to do good design.
Do not compromise, regardless of budget, criticism or other obstacles.
Do not ever believe someone who uses the words 'good enough'.
Do not stop thinking of ways to make an improvement to something,
even on press, even in the bindery or even the next day.

Client –
Listen to the client, incorporate their ideas; they know their business.

Studio –
Support your colleagues; good design is hard to do.

Account Managers –
They are helpful.
Try to listen to what they are telling you.
Do not take art direction from them. When it comes to art direction, if the sentence starts with
"the client said...", stop listening immediately.

Production –
Always find time to answer production questions.
Always give the correct answer. Unlike design, not a good place for guessing.
Encourage production to be relentlessly critical of details

Vendors –
Try to keep in mind that there is no way to work without them, but do not take statements that begin
with the words "we can't do that" seriously.
Never assume anything when it comes to vendors. You must say every little thing aloud, and with at least one witness
When they say something you don't understand, just say "you'll have to run that one by Steve"

General –
Try to keep your desk clean.
Do not accumulate junk under your desk.
Try not to freak out when Steve rummages around in your drawers.
Do not get freelance deliveries at the studio.
Try not to take some things too personally. Like things that are said during a Marathon game.
Remember: design is fun! And keep saying, over and over, the Tolleson motto..."there are no bad projects."

published by
Princeton Architectural Press
37 East 7th Street, New York, NY 10003
212.995.9620

© 1999 Tolleson Design
isbn 1-56898-198-8

03 02 01 00   5 4 3 2
Printed in Hong Kong.

Project Editor: Therese Kelly
Special thanks to everyone in my studio: Jean Orlebeke, Gabriella Rossi, Holly Hudson,
Ellen Elfering, Mark Winn, Bill Bowers, John Barretto, Helena Wallentén, Mary Wall,
Sarah White, René Rosso, Craig Clark, and Lindsay Beaman.
For a free catalog of books published by Princeton Architectural Press,
call 800.722.6657 or visit www.papress.com.

Tolleson, Steven, 1957-
    Soak, wash, rinse, spin. Tolleson Design / Steven Tolleson
        p.   cm.
        ISBN 1-56898-198-8 (alk. paper)
        1. Tolleson Design (Firm) 2. Commercial art–California–San
    Francisco–History–20th century. 3. Design–Methodology.
    I. Title.
    NC999.4.T84A4   1999
    741.6'0973–dc21   99-38219
                                                                       CIP

6/1998 - 6.28.99 :

90 mtgs.

4.1.99 - 6.28.99 :

4320 fl.oz. coffee

2880 fl.oz. pepsi

2880 fl.oz. diet pepsi

1 clove cig.

800 drops of kava kava

2 bladder infections

2089 hours at the studio

8 parking tickets

58 ny - sf phone calls

1 plane ticket to hong kong